MW01193829

The
1865
CUSTOMS of SERVICE

FOR

NON-COMMISSIONED OFFICERS AND SOLDIERS

BY

AUGUST V. KAUTZ,
CAPT. SIXTH U.S. CAVALRY, BRIG.-GEN. U.S. VOLUNTEERS.

SECOND EDITION.

STACKPOLE
BOOKS

Published by
STACKPOLE BOOKS
5067 Ritter Road
Mechanicsburg, Pa. 17055
www.stackpolebooks.com

Cover design by Wendy Reynolds

10 9 8 7 6 5 4 3

First Stackpole Edition

Library of Congress Cataloging-in-Publication Data

Kautz, August V. (August Valentine), 1828–1895.
    [Customs of service for non-commissioned officers and soldiers]
    The 1865 customs of service for non-commissioned officers and
soldiers / by August V. Kautz.— 1st Stackpole ed.
        p. cm.
    Originally published as: Customs of service for non-comissioned
officers and soldiers as derived from law and regulations and
practised in the Army of the United States : being a hand-book ...
2nd ed. Philadelphia : Lippincott, 1865.
    Includes index.
    ISBN 0-8117-0399-1 (alk. paper)
    1. United States. Army—Handbooks, manuals, etc.
    2. United States.
Army—Non-commissioned officers' handbooks. I. Title.

U113.K21 2001
355.3'38'0973—dc21

                                                    00-051585

CUSTOMS OF SERVICE

FOR

NON-COMMISSIONED OFFICERS AND SOLDIERS

AS

Derived from Law and Regulations

AND

PRACTISED IN THE ARMY OF THE UNITED STATES

BEING

A HAND-BOOK FOR THE RANK AND FILE OF THE ARMY
SHOWING WHAT ARE THE RIGHTS AND DUTIES,
HOW TO OBTAIN THE FORMER AND PERFORM
THE LATTER, AND THEREBY ENABLING
THEM TO SEEK PROMOTION AND
DISTINCTION IN THE SERVICE OF THEIR COUNTRY.

BY

AUGUST V. KAUTZ,

CAPT. SIXTH U.S. CAVALRY, BRIG.-GEN. U.S. VOLUNTEERS.

SECOND EDITION.

1865.

PREFACE.

THE individual instruction of the soldier is the foundation upon which the structure of the army rests. If it is complete, the operations of the army, aided by military science, may be calculated with mathematical accuracy; and unless it is carried to a certain point at least, the management of an army is a mere matter of chance, and success the result only of fortuitous circumstances. Whilst able men have devoted themselves to the higher branches of the military profession, it is a matter of great surprise that the rudiments have been so long overlooked.

Heretofore the enlisted soldier has been dependent upon tradition for a knowledge of his specific duties; for justice he has been at the mercy of his superiors.

If his officers were competent and conscientious men, faithful in the discharge of their duties and industrious in accumulating and disseminating knowledge among the men, they were cared for, their rights were secured to them, and the ambitious and meritorious were enabled to obtain advancement.

On the contrary, if their superiors were incompetent and unscrupulous men, careless in the execution of their duties, and indolent in acquiring knowledge and instructing the soldiers, the latter were neglected, their rights suffered, and they had little or no opportunity of learning those things necessary to their advancement.

Confident that every soldier who is desirous of learning his duties will feel grateful for this little volume, the author places before them the means of studying for themselves what they so much desire to know.

Once a private himself, in the 1st Ohio Regiment, in the Mexican War, he has by a continuous service since that period been enabled, through his own varied experience, to select the most valuable, if not all the important, information necessary for every grade of the enlisted men. If they are by this means enabled to feel independent of their officers in acquiring a knowledge of their own duties, the highest aim of the book will be attained. Although prepared for the soldiers of the regular army, it is equally applicable to the volunteer service, except in some few cases that are fully explained.

LIST OF ABBREVIATIONS

USED IN THIS BOOK AND IN OTHER MILITARY WORKS,
AND IN MAKING OUT OFFICIAL PAPERS.

A. A. A. G.—Acting Assistant Adjutant-General.

A. A. G.—Assistant Adjutant-General.

A. A. Q. M.—Acting Assistant Quartermaster.

A. C. S.—Acting Commissary of Subsistence.

A. D. C.—Aid-de-camp.

A. G. O.—Adjutant-General's Office.

Act March 3, 1863.—Act of Congress approved March 3, 1863.

Adjt.—Adjutant.

Art.—Artillery.

Art. 35.—Thirty-Fifth Article of War.

Asst.—Assistant.

A. I. G.—Assistant Inspector-General.

Bat.—Battalion.

Batry.—Battery.

Brig.—Brigadier, Brigade.

Bug.—Bugler.

Bur.—Bureau.

Bvt.—Brevet.

C. S.—Commissary of Subsistence.

Capt.—Captain.

Cav.—Cavalry.

Cdt.—Cadet.

Chap.—Chaplain.

Co.—Company.

Col.—Colonel.

Comdg.—Commanding.

Comdt.—Commandant.

Corp.—Corporal.

Dept.—Department.

Det.—Detachment.

Div.—Division.

Drag.—Dragoon.

Eng.—Engineer.

Ens.—Ensign.

Far.—Farrier.

Ft.-Fort.

G. O.—General Order.

Gen.—General.

Hd.-Qrs.—Head-Quarters.

Hosp.—Hospital.

Hosp. Stwd.—Hospital Steward.

Inf.—Infantry.

Inspr.—Inspector.

I. G.—Inspector-General.

J. Advt.—Judge-Advocate.

L. Art.—Light Artillery.
Lieut. and Lt.—Lieutenant.

M. R.—Mounted Rifles.
M. S.—Medical Staff.
M. S. K.—Military Store-keeper.
Maj.—Major.
Med. Cdt.—Medical Cadet.
Med. Dept.—Medical Department.

N. C. O.—Non-commissioned Officer.

O. B.—Official Business.
Ord.—Ordnance.
Ord. Sergt.—Ordnance Sergeant.

P. D.—Pay Department.
P. M.—Paymaster.
Par.—Paragraph.
Pvt.—Private.

Q. M.—Quartermaster.
Qrs.—Quarters.

R. C. S.—Regimental Commissary of Subsistence.
R. Q. M.—Regimental Quartermaster.
Rct.—Recruit.
Reg.—In this book, Revised *Regulations* of 1863.

Regt.—Regiment.
Regtl.—Regimental.

S. O.—Special Order, Signal Officer.
Sdlr.—Saddler.
Sec.—Section.
Sergt.—Sergeant.
Sergt. Maj.—Sergeant-Major.
Servt.—Servant.
Sub. Dept.—Subsistence Department.
Supt.—Superintendent.
Surg.—Surgeon.
Surg. M.—Surgeon's Mate.

Top. Eng.—Topographical Engineer.
Trptr.—Trumpeter.

U. S. A.—United States Army.
U. S. Art.—United States Artillery.
U. S. Cav.—United States Cavalry.
U. S. Eng.—United States Engineers.
U. S. I.—United States Infantry.
U. S. M. D.—United States Medical Department.
U. S. T. Eng.—United States Topographical Engineers.

Vol.—Volunteers.
Vouch.—Voucher.

W. D.—War Department.

CUSTOMS OF SERVICE

FOR

NON-COMMISSIONED OFFICERS AND SOLDIERS.

THE SOLDIER.

1. THE soldier commands respect in proportion to his capacity and length of service. A youth of military pride and bearing, who wears his uniform with neatness and grace, and does his duty faithfully and with energy and determination, deserves admiration, and generally receives it; but the veteran whose scars and wounds are the reminders of many battles, and whose numerous service-chevrons and gray hairs mark a life devoted to the service of his country, chains the listening ear of the citizen to the story of his heroic life, and the greatest chieftain will raise his hat with respect to return his punctilious salute.

2. The decisive events of a soldier's life are few and far between, and the intervals are devoted to waiting for these turning-points. If the time he

spends in waiting is usually occupied in preparing himself for the critical moments, he will thereby enhance his chances of success, and add lustre to the promotion which his achievements are sure to obtain for him.

3. The military profession involves a knowledge of almost every art, and information accumulated and held in store for the fortunate moment is suddenly demanded and called for, and he who can come forward and say, "I possess it," is the victor. A soldier can, therefore, never be placed in any situation in which his leisure moments may not be devoted to something that may some time win him a grade.

4. All knowledge, however, is the more readily obtained if sought after methodically. Thus, a soldier should be conversant first of all with the proper and legitimate duties of his grade, and, these attained, his next step is the acquirement of a knowledge of the duties of the next highest position; for success in military life is usually a succession of progressive steps from a lower to a higher, and the omission of one of these steps is an important deficiency, that should be repaired as soon as possible. Those officers who undertake the duties of a position without having made themselves familiar with those of grades below them are at a great disadvantage.

5. Beginning at the moment the soldier enters the ranks, we shall endeavor to make known to him

all his duties in detail, in the order in which they
are likely to be required of him, up to the grade of a
commissioned officer.

THE PRIVATE SOLDIER.

6. In the fullest sense, any man in the military
service who receives pay, whether sworn in or not,
is a soldier, because he is subject to military law.
Under this general head, laborers, teamsters, sutlers, chaplains, &c. are soldiers. In a more limited
sense, a private soldier is a man enlisted in the military service to serve in the cavalry, artillery, or infantry. He is said to be enlisted when he has been
examined, his duties of obedience explained to
him, and after he has taken the prescribed oath.

7. "Any free white* male person above the age
of eighteen, and under thirty-five years of age,
being at least five feet three inches high; effective,
able-bodied, sober, free from disease, of good character and habits, and with a competent knowledge
of the English language, may be enlisted as a soldier." (Reg. 929.) This regulation makes exceptions
in favor of musicians and soldiers who have served

---

*The enlistment of negroes and Indians is a peculiarity
of the volunteer service, and has not yet been authorized
for the regular service.

one enlistment, although they should be under the prescribed height and age. A soldier cannot claim a discharge in consequence of any defect in the above requirements, unless, in case of a minor, he can prove that the requirements of the law have not been complied with in his enlistment.

8. In case of a minor under eighteen years of age, the written consent of the parents or guardian must be appended.

9. In time of peace, married men are excluded from enlistment, except in cases of re-enlistment, except by special authority from the Adjutant-General's Office. (Reg. 930.) It is but just to the soldier to know that his being such does not exclude him from getting married, or annul in any way the marriage contract. At the same time, he cannot claim exemption from any duty because he is married.

10. Whilst it is impossible for an officer to prevent a soldier from getting married, it is recommended, if he wishes to do so, that he should procure the consent of the company commander; otherwise he may subject himself to great unhappiness, as the officer is not required to recognize the wife in the army, and no provision is made for her; she cannot claim quarters or subsistence, nor any exemption for her husband from the duties of the soldier on her account.

11. Four laundresses are allowed to each company, and soldiers' wives may be, and generally are, mustered in that capacity. They are then entitled to

the same quarters, fuel, and rations as a soldier, and the established pay for the washing they may do for soldiers and officers.

12. The term of enlistment at present in the regular service is for three years. In the volunteer service it varies according to the call under which they enter service. (Act July 29, 1861, sec. 5.)

13. After enlistment, no soldier can be discharged before the expiration of his term of service, except by order of the President, the Secretary of War, the commanding officer of a department in case of disability, or the sentence of a general court-martial. (Art. 11.) No soldier can leave the service without a proper discharge, without subjecting himself to the penalty of desertion. Any soldier who leaves his command, without permission, more than one mile, subjects himself to the penalty of desertion. (Art. 41.)

14. Any officer of the regular army is authorized to administer the oath to a soldier upon his enlistment. (Act Aug. 3, 1861, sec. 11.)

15. Whilst officers are required to have the Articles of War read to soldiers, no soldier can plead, in bar of punishment, that this regulation has not been complied with, although he may plead it in extenuation of his offence. Soldiers are not subject to arrest for debt, except where the sum is twenty dollars, or more, and then it must be contracted before enlisting. (Act Jan. 11, 1812.)

16. "Every soldier who, having been honorably

discharged from the service of the United States, shall, within one month thereafter, re-enlist, shall be entitled to two dollars per month in addition to the ordinary pay of his grade, for the first period of five years after the expiration of his previous enlistment, and a further sum of one dollar per month for each successive period of five years, so long as he shall remain continuously in the army." (Act Aug. 4, 1854, sec. 3.)

17. Soldiers who served in the war with Mexico, and received a "Certificate of Merit" for distinguished services, shall receive two dollars per month, to which that certificate would have entitled them had they remained continuously in the service." (Ib. sec. 3.)

18. Non-commissioned officers who were recommended for promotion by brevet to the lowest grade of commissioned officers, but did not receive the benefit of that provision (Act March 3, 1847, sec. 17), shall be entitled to the additional pay authorized to be given to such privates as received certificates of merit. (Ib. sec. 4.)

PAY AND ALLOWANCES OF SOLDIERS.

19. THE pay and allowances of soldiers vary somewhat at different times, under different circumstances, and in different arms of service.

20. The pay of the private soldier in the cavalry, artillery and infantry, as fixed by law, is sixteen dollars per month. (Act June 20, 1864.) One dollar per month of the soldier's pay is retained monthly by the paymaster, to be paid upon the expiration of his enlistment.

21. Non-commissioned officers and musicians do not have any of their pay retained, except for the period in which they have served or may serve as privates.

22. Twelve and one-half cents is deducted from the pay of all enlisted men per month by the paymaster, for the support of the Military Asylum or Soldiers' Home. (Act March 3, 1859, sec. 7.)

23. The soldier has an annual allowance for clothing, the amount of which is obtained by computing the cost of the average amount of clothing allowed to soldiers for the year. (Reg. 1157.) This allowance is published periodically in orders by the War Department, in connection with the prices of clothing.

24. The first sergeant of the company keeps the clothing account of the soldier, under the direction of the company commander. After each issue, the money value of all the clothing drawn should be entered on it, and the soldier's signature obtained to its correctness. Should the soldier not draw the amount of clothing allowed in kind, it may be commuted, and the balance paid in money on the expiration of his term of enlistment.

25. At the end of each year, the difference saved is carried to his credit, and paid him in money at the expiration of his term of enlistment. (Reg. 1150.) Should he exceed the amount in any year, it is charged on the next subsequent muster roll and deducted from his pay by the paymaster. (Reg. 1155.)

26. A soldier who re-enlists within one month after or two months before the expiration of his enlistment, is entitled to two dollars per month additional for re-enlistment, and one dollar per month for each subsequent period of five years' service.

27. Bounties are generally allowed to soldiers, which are sometimes directed by law, and sometimes by orders from the War Department. States often offer bounties to volunteers. The time and manner of payment are prescribed by orders from the War Department. The bounties allowed by States to volunteers are generally of local notoriety.

28. General Order No. 190, dated War Department, June 25, 1863, authorized a premium, advance pay, and bounty to all men who would enlist before the 1st of December, 1863 (G. O. 338), in the regular army, the enlistment being for five years, as follows, viz.:

Premium paid on enlistment $2 00
Advance pay, first payment after muster 13 00
Advance bounty, paid at depot after being accepted . . 25 00

Total $40 00

Bounty to be paid at the second regular pay-day
  after enlistment $50 00
Bounty to be paid at first pay-day after 8 months'
  service 50 00
Bounty to be paid at first pay-day after 12 months'
  service 50 00
Bounty to be paid at first pay-day after 2 years'
  service 50 00
Bounty to be paid at first pay-day after 3 years'
  service 50 00
Bounty to be paid at first pay-day after 4 years'
  service 50 00
Bounty to be paid at the expiration of service 75 00

29. This bounty of four hundred dollars, by the
same order, was extended to all soldiers then in
service in the regular army, whose terms would expire within one year, and who re-enlisted within
two months before the expiration of their term of
service.

30. General Order No. 191, of the same date as
the foregoing, extended a similar bounty to veteran
volunteers, the enlistment being for three years or
during the war. All those who enlisted between the
25th of June and the 1st of December, 1863, although not previously in service (G. 0. 324), and all
those who re-enlisted subsequent to the order, after
at least nine months' service, are entitled as follows, viz.:

Upon being mustered into service, one month's pay
    in advance $13 00
Also first instalment of bounty 60 00
Also premium................................... 2 00

       Total payment on muster $75 00

At the first regular pay-day, or 2 months after
    muster in $50 00
At the first regular pay-day after 6 months'
    service 50 00
At the first regular pay-day after 12 months'
    service 50 00
At the first regular pay-day after 18 months'
    service 50 00
At the first regular pay-day after 2 years' service   50 00
At the first regular pay-day after 2 1/2 years' service   50 00
At the expiration of 3 years' service, the remainder   40 00

31. Should the war end before the expiration of
their enlistment, volunteers will nevertheless receive the remainder of the four hundred dollars;
and should the soldier die in service, the heir will
receive the balance due.

32. Soldiers have the privilege of depositing
money in the hands of the paymaster for safe keeping, provided that the amount deposited at any one
time is not less than five dollars, and that it shall
not be withdrawn before the expiration of the soldier's enlistment. (Reg. 1354.) A checkbook is given
the soldier, and a certificate of each deposit is entered and signed by the paymaster.

33. The company commander must keep an ac-

count of each deposit in the Descriptive Book, and after each payment transmit a list of the depositors and the amounts to the Paymaster-General. In case of transfer, the amount of the deposit is entered on the soldier's descriptive roll.

34. When discharged, they are entered on his final statements; and when a soldier dies, the amount of his deposit is entered on the inventory. These deposits are not liable to forfeiture by sentence of a court-martial, and are secure to the soldier or his heirs against all accident.

35. A soldier is entitled to one ration per day. During the present war, the ration is very ample. The rations are drawn in bulk by the company commander, and distributed under his direction to the company.

36. A soldier serving away from his company, and it being impracticable to draw his rations or to carry them with him, the commissary may commute them at seventy-five cents per day when due, or in advance on the order of the commanding officer. (Reg. 1216.)

37. This contemplates services for short periods, such as carrying expresses, pursuit of deserters, &c.; and where soldiers are placed on duty in a situation where subsistence is unusually expensive it would no doubt be allowed. Otherwise, on furlough or on duty, where rations cannot be issued in kind, they will be commuted at the cost price of the place or station. (Reg. 1218.)

38. When a soldier is discharged, he is allowed pay for the number of days from the post where discharged to the place of his enlistment, at the rate of twenty miles per day, and a ration for each day, which is commuted at the cost price of a ration at the post where discharged.

39. In cases of "excessive fatigue" or "severe exposure," soldiers may receive an issue of whiskey of one gill per ration.

40. By the Act of March 3, 1863, sec. 35, extra-duty pay to soldiers is discontinued, and enlisted men detailed to special service cannot receive any extra pay for such service beyond that allowed other enlisted men of the same grade.[*]

41. The authorized farriers, saddlers, wagoners, blacksmiths, and artificers allowed for cavalry and artillery have salaries fixed by law,—viz.: artificers, farriers, and blacksmiths, eighteen dollars; saddlers and wagoners, fourteen dollars. The extra pay formerly allowed is therefore prohibited.

42. Soldiers detailed as hospital nurses, attendants, and cooks are not allowed any additional pay, as heretofore. Soldiers detailed on extra duty as stewards in hospitals cannot receive the thirty dollars allowed to hospital stewards until their appointment has been approved by the Surgeon-Gene-

---

[*]The decision of the Third Auditor is, that until the Regulation authorizing extra pay is rescinded, extra pay may be allowed.

ral, and they have been transferred from the line to the Medical department.

43. It has been the practice of the Government to extend to soldiers who have served in any of the wars certain other allowances, either of extra pay or land-warrants; also medals for distinguished services rendered.

44. The law also provides for disabled soldiers who have been rendered so in the line of their duty, by giving them pensions. For total disability the pension allowed for non-commissioned officers, musicians, and privates is eight dollars per month. In case of death from wounds or disease, the widow, or, if no widow, the legitimate children under sixteen, or, if no widow or children, a dependent mother, and, if neither widow, children, nor mother, an orphan sister or sisters, dependent, and under sixteen years of age, are entitled to the pension.

45. The Military Asylum, or Soldiers' Home, is an institution created for the benefit of indigent, superannuated, and disabled soldiers, where they are clothed, subsisted, and taken care of at public expense. The institution is open to all soldiers who have become unfit for service, in the service of the United States. It is one of the richest and best-endowed institutions in the United States, it a healthy and pleasant locality about two or three miles north of Washington, in the District of Columbia.

46. Soldiers who become insane in the service

are provided for and sent to the Asylum for the Insane at Washington.

DUTIES OF THE SOLDIER.

DEPORTMENT.

47. ONE of the first things a soldier has to learn on entering the army, is a proper military deportment towards his superiors in rank: this is nothing more than the military way of performing the courtesies required from a well-bred man in civil life, and a punctual performance of them is as much to his credit as the observance of the ordinary rules of common politeness.

48. "Sergeants, with swords drawn, will salute by bringing them to a present; with muskets, by bringing the left hand across the body, so as to strike the musket near the right shoulder. Corporals out of the ranks, and privates not sentries, will carry their muskets at a shoulder as sergeants, and salute in like manner." (Reg. 255.)

49. "When a soldier without arms, or with side-arms only, meets an officer, he is to raise his hand to the right side of the visor of his cap, palm to the front, elbow raised as high as the shoulder, looking at the same time in a respectful and soldier-like manner at the officer, who will return the compliment thus offered." (Reg. 256.)

50. "A non-commissioned officer or soldier being seated, and without particular occupation, will rise on the approach of an officer, and make the customary salutation. If standing, he will turn toward the officer for the same purpose. If the parties remain in the same place or on the same ground, such compliments need not be repeated." (Reg. 257.)

51. The foregoing regulations should be strictly observed by enlisted men; and their faithful performance will add much to the military reputation of a company or regiment.

52. The following customs are equally binding, though not provided for in Regulations:—

When soldiers are marching in the ranks, they do not salute, unless ordered at the time. If employed at any work, they are not expected to discontinue their employment to salute.

53. A soldier or non-commissioned officer, when he addresses an officer, or is spoken to by one, salutes; on receiving the answer or communication from the officer, he again salutes before turning to go away.

54. When a soldier enters an officer's quarters armed, he simply makes the required salute, and does not take off his cap; but without arms, or with side-arms only, he takes off his cap and stands in the position of a soldier, and delivers his message or communicates what he came for in as few words as possible and to the point.

55. A slovenly attitude, frequent changes of position, or much gesticulation, is exceedingly unmilitary, and looks bad. Say what you have to say in a prompt, courageous manner, without diffidence or hesitation; and, if always respectful, no matter what the subject, it is much more likely to be considered than when delivered in a drawling, hesitating, and timid manner.

56. A mounted soldier should always dismount if the officer he wishes to address is dismounted. A mounted soldier passing an officer salutes with the hand, except when he has his sabre drawn, and then he salutes with the sabre.

57. When a soldier enters an officer's quarters, he remains standing in the position of a soldier until invited to sit down. When soldiers are in a room and an officer enters, they should rise and remain standing until invited to sit down.

58. Soldiers should bear in mind that the officer has his duties to perform, and that they are more weighty and important than any soldier can have, and that his leisure time is limited, and they should therefore avoid, as much as possible, troubling him with unimportant matters, or, at least, not be disappointed if they receive short answers.

59. In a company of seventy or eighty men, if each one should go only once a day to his captain with any matter, it is easily seen how annoying such a thing would soon become.

60. Soldiers should learn, as far as possible, to

manage their own affairs; and, whilst their company commander is the legitimate person to apply to for any thing needful or when in difficulty, his time should not be trespassed upon with regard to matters they should know themselves.

61. The company commander, through the first sergeant, is the proper person to apply to for all indulgences, such as passes, furloughs, &c., and for clothing, rations, pay, and the adjustment of all differences and difficulties in the company.

62. An application to any other source will most generally be answered by referring the applicant to his company commander, whose duty it is to attend to the wants of his men. Only when the company commander neglects his duty in this respect is a soldier justified in applying to his regimental or post commander.

INSTRUCTION.

63. The first duties which a newly-enlisted soldier is called upon to perform are to familiarize himself with his camp or garrison duties.

64. He is provided with clothing, which he is expected to adapt to the best advantage to improve his military appearance, by the best means in his power. There is usually a tailor or two in the company or among the recruits, who is excused from all duty possible, to fit soldiers' clothing for a moderate compensation.

65. Under the instruction of a drill-sergeant, he

is taught the first principles in the "School of the Soldier." After a certain progress in the instruction without arms, his arms and accoutrements are issued to him; for these he is held responsible, and, if injured or lost by any fault of his, they are charged to him on his muster-roll, and their value deducted from his pay at the first subsequent payment.

66. Should the arms or accoutrements be lost or destroyed or injured in any way not the fault of the soldier, the commanding officer may order a board of survey, who, if the facts authorize it, may relieve the soldier from the payment.

67. The soldier's instruction is usually completed at the depot for recruits, before the recruit reaches his company; if not, it is continued when he joins it. After he is fully instructed in the "School of the Soldier," he is ready to be placed in the company ranks.

68. This is the usual course pursued with the soldier in the regular army, and, as far as possible, it should be followed with volunteers and militia. But, as they are usually called into service for special purposes and on sudden emergencies, the same thoroughness cannot be attained, and is not expected.

69. The duties of the thoroughly-instructed soldier partake of two kinds, depending upon whether he is in a garrison or camp of instruction or other

camp, and in the field in front of the enemy in time of war.

DUTIES IN CAMP OR GARRISON.

70. It is the duty of the soldier, under all circumstances, to be always present with his company for duty, and attend all the standing roll-calls and exercises, unless specially excused by his commanding officer, or he is sick and excused by the surgeon, or is absent on duty.

71. The various duties to which a soldier is subject are matters of regular detail,—each soldier taking his regular tour of each as it comes,—and consist, in the main, of the following:—

1st. Guards. 2d. Working-parties, or Fatigue. 3d. Daily duty.

72. The roster for these various details is kept by the first sergeant, and the longest off are the first to be detailed. The details are usually published to the company at retreat roll-call for the next day.

73. At the hour fixed, the detail is paraded for the duty by the first sergeant on the company parade-ground, and marched to the parade-ground or rendezvous for such parties, and received by the sergeant-major or adjutant, who inspects the guard or party, and, after all the details have arrived, sees that they are properly equipped as required, and then turns the detachment over to the officer detailed

to take charge of it, who immediately proceeds to march it to the performance of the duty required.

74. For guard, the form and ceremony are prescribed in Regulations. (Reg. 375 to 398.) A soldier cannot leave his guard or party, until regularly relieved or marched off, without permission from his superior officer. (Articles of War 44 and 50.)

75. ON GUARD.—When the guard has marched on, it is divided into three reliefs, and in each relief the soldier is numbered, and he retains his number and the same relief during his tour, unless specially changed.

76. When the soldier is placed upon post, he becomes a sentinel; his duties then are of two distinct characters,—those which belong to all sentinels on all posts, and those peculiar to the post on which he is placed. The former are called *general*, and the latter *special*.

77. When called upon by the commanding officer, the officer of the day, or some officer or noncommissioned officer of the guard, to give his orders, he does so, in substance, in the following general terms, which he should understand sufficiently well to explain in detail, viz.:—

78. "I am required to take charge of this post and all public property in view; to salute all officers passing, according to rank; to give the alarm in case of fire, or the approach of an enemy, or any disturbance whatsoever; to report all violations of

the Articles of War, Regulations of the Army, or camp or garrison orders; at night, to challenge all persons approaching my post, and to allow no one to pass without the countersign until they are examined by an officer or non-commissioned officer of the guard."

79. "My special orders are" (*here state them as they are given, as when in charge of commissary or quartermaster's stores*) "to take charge of all these stores, and to allow no one to interfere with or take them away, except by direction of the quartermaster or commissary sergeant, or the quartermaster or commissary himself."

80. He should know what is meant by the above, and be able to explain it in detail.

Thus, to take charge of his post means to walk diligently the length of his beat, the limits of which are generally indicated to him; to take charge of all public property in view is to prevent, if possible, any damage being done to houses, fences, tents, trees, &c., by any unauthorized persons: if he cannot do so without leaving his post, he calls out for the corporal of the guard, and his number, and reports the matter to him.

81. To salute all officers, according to rank, who may pass near his post, means to halt and face outwards, and stand at a "carry," until the officer has passed, if the officer is of the rank of captain or below; if above the rank of captain, the sentinel must "present arms." He must, also, "present arms"

to the *officer of the day* and *commanding officer*, whether above or below the rank of captain.

82. This involves a knowledge of the uniforms of officers. A safe guide is the fact that all officers above the rank of captain in the army have a double row of buttons on their coats, whilst captains and lieutenants have only a single row.[*]

83. Armed bodies of men passing near the sentinel's post, commanded by an officer, are entitled to a "present;" if under a non-commissioned officer, they are saluted with a "carry." To give the alarm is to call out "the guard," to fire off his piece, or to cry "fire."

84. To report all violations of camp or garrison orders, or Regulations, or of the Articles of War, is to call the corporal of the guard and report the facts to him. This includes all the irregularities usually prohibited among troops, such as discharging fire-arms, committing nuisance, drunkenness, disorderly conduct, sale of liquor, gambling, improper or excluded characters, and, in general, every thing that is known to be prohibited or improper.

85. To challenge is to call out, "Who comes there?" Soldiers usually commence challenging after *taps*, and continue until reveille; although it

---

*Note.—Officers of the Navy at a short distance cannot be recognized by this means, as they all have double rows of buttons.

is sometimes ordered to commence challenging immediately after retreat.

86. No. 1 sentinel is always posted at the house, tent, or bivouac where the guard is quartered. His beat is always in front of the guard, and his duties are mostly *special*. The prisoners are more or less under his charge. He salutes officers passing, as on other posts; but, in addition, he calls, "Turn out the guard," for the officer of the day, *commanding officer*, and all *general officers* and all *bodies of troops* approaching, and announces at the same time who approaches. "He reports violations as other sentinels, but does not receive the countersign; but, challenging at night, he commands, "halt," and calls, "Corporal of the guard," and repeats the answer received. If the officer of the day or any one entitled to the compliment, he commands, "Halt; *turn out the guard, officer of the day!*"

87. The other sentinels of the guard are posted according to numbers, and in the order most convenient for going from and returning to the guard. They are generally posted two hours on and four hours off.

88. The following Regulations are sufficiently clear and distinct without explanation:—

"399. Sentinels will be relieved every two hours, unless the state of the weather, or other causes, should make it necessary or proper that it be done at shorter or longer intervals.

"400. Each relief, before mounting, is inspected by the

commander of the guard or of its post. The corporal reports to him, and presents the old relief on its return.

"401. The *countersign* or watchword, is given to such persons as are entitled to pass during the night, and to officers, non-commissioned officers, and sentinels of the guard. Interior guards receive the countersign only when ordered by the commander of the troops.

"402. The *parole* is imparted to such officers only as have a right to visit the guards, and to make the grand rounds; and to officers commanding guards.

"403. As soon as the new guard has been marched off, the officer of the day will repair to the office of the commanding officer and report for orders.

"404. The officer of the day must see that the officer of the guard is furnished with the parole and countersign before *retreat*.

"405. The officer of the day visits the guards during the day at such times as he may deem necessary, and makes his rounds at night at least once after 12 o'clock.

"406. Upon being relieved, the officer of the day will make such remarks in the report of the officer of the guard as circumstances require, and present the same at headquarters.

"407. Commanders of guards leaving their posts to visit their sentinels, or on other duty, are to mention their intention, and the probable time of their absence, to the next in command.

"408. The officers are to remain constantly at their guards, except while visiting their sentinels, or necessarily engaged elsewhere on their proper duty.

"409. Neither officers nor soldiers are to take off their clothing or accoutrements while they are on guard.

"410. The officer of the guard must see that the counter

sign is duly communicated to the sentinels a little before twilight.

"411. When a fire breaks out, or any alarm is raised in a garrison, all guards are to be immediately under arms.

"412. Inexperienced officers are put on guard as supernumeraries, for the purpose of instruction.

"413. Sentinels will not take orders or allow themselves to be relieved, except by an officer or non-commissioned officer of their guard or party, the officer of the day, or the commanding officer; in which case the orders will be immediately notified to the commander of the guard by the officer giving them.

"414. Sentinels will report every breach of orders or regulations they are instructed to enforce.

"415. Sentinels must keep themselves on the alert, observing every thing that takes place within sight and hearing of their post. They will carry their arms habitually at support, or on either shoulder, but will never quit them. In wet weather, if there be no sentry-box, they will secure arms.

"416. No sentinel shall quit his post or hold conversation not necessary to the proper discharge of his duty.

"417. All persons, of whatever rank in the service, are required to observe respect toward sentinels.

"418. In case of disorder, a sentinel must call out *the guard;* and if a fire take place, he must cry—*'Fire!'* adding the number of his post. If in either case, the danger be great, he must discharge his firelock before calling out.

"419. It is the duty of a sentinel to repeat all calls made from posts more distant from the main body of the guard than his own, and no sentinel will be posted so distant as not to be heard by the guard, either directly or through other sentinels.

"420. Sentinels will present arms to general and field

officers, to the officer of the day, and to the commanding officer of the post. To all other officers they will carry arms.

"421. When a sentinel in his sentry-box sees an officer approaching, he will stand at *attention*, and as the officer passes will salute him, by bringing the left hand briskly to the musket, as high as the right shoulder.

"422. The sentinel at any post of the guard, when he sees any body of troops, or an officer entitled to compliment, approach, must call—'*Turn out the guard!*' and announce who approaches.

"423. Guards do not turn out as a matter of compliment after sunset; but sentinels will, when officers in uniform approach, pay them proper attention, by facing to the proper front, and standing steady at *shouldered arms.* This will be observed until the evening is so far advanced that the sentinels begin challenging.

"424. After retreat (or the hour appointed by the commanding officer), until broad daylight, a sentinel challenges every person who approaches him, taking, at the same time, the position of *arms port.* He will suffer no person to come nearer than within reach of his bayonet, until the person has given the countersign.

"425. A sentinel, in challenging, will call out—'*Who comes there?*' If answered—'*Friend, with the countersign,*' and he be instructed to pass persons with the countersign, he will reply—'Advance, friend, with the countersign!' If answered—'*Friends!*' he will reply—'*Halt, friends! Advance one with the countersign!*' If answered—'*Relief,*' '*Patrol,*' or '*Grand rounds,*' he will reply—'*Halt! Advance, Sergeant (or Corporal), with the countersign!*' and satisfy himself that the party is what it represents itself to be. If he have no authority to pass persons with the countersign, if the wrong countersign be given, or if the persons have not the countersign, he will cause them to stand, and call—'*Corporal of the guard!*'

"426. In the daytime, when the sentinel before the guard sees the officer of the day approach, he will call—'*Turn out the guard! officer of the day.*' The guard will be paraded, and salute with presented arms.

"427. When any person approaches a post of the guard at night, the sentinel before the post, after challenging, causes him to halt until examined by a non-commissioned officer of the guard. If it be the officer of the day, or any other officer entitled to inspect the guard and to make the rounds, the non-commissioned officer will call—'*Turn out the guard!*' when the guard will be paraded at shouldered arms, and the officer of the guard, if he thinks necessary, may demand the countersign and parole.

"428. The officer of the day, wishing to make the rounds, will take an escort of a non-commissioned officer and two men. When the rounds are challenged by a sentinel, the sergeant will answer—'*Grand rounds!*' and the sentinel will reply—'*Halt, grand rounds! Advance, sergeant, with the countersign!*' Upon which the sergeant advances and gives the countersign. The sentinel will then cry—'*Advance, rounds!*' and stand at a shoulder till they have passed.

"429. When the sentinel before the guard challenges, and is answered—'*Grand rounds,*' he will reply—'*Halt, grand rounds! Turn out the guard; grand rounds!*' Upon which the guard will be drawn up at shouldered arms. The officer commanding the guard will then order a sergeant and two men to advance; when within ten paces, the sergeant challenges. The sergeant of the grand rounds answers—'*Grand rounds!*' The sergeant of the guard replies—'*Advance, sergeant, with the countersign!*' The sergeant of the rounds advances alone, gives the countersign, and returns to his round. The sergeant of the guard calls to his officer—'*The countersign is right!*' on which the officer of the guard calls—'*Advance, rounds!*' The officer of the rounds then advances alone, the guard standing at shouldered arms. The officer of the rounds passes along the front of the guard to the officer, who keeps his post on the right, and gives him the parole. He then examines the guard, orders back his escort, and, taking a new one, proceeds in the same manner to other guards.

"430. All material instructions given to a sentinel on post by persons entitled to make grand rounds, ought to be promptly notified to the commander of the guard.

"431. Any general officer, or the commander of a post or garrison, may visit the guards of his command, and go the grand rounds, and be received in the same manner as prescribed for the officer of the day."

89. Sentinels must be respected under all circumstances and should not be held responsible for orders they execute in good faith; and no officers have authority to interfere with them, except as provided in par. 413, Army Regulations.

90. Sentinels are often, even in times of peace, placed in trying and difficult positions. In times of popular excitement, they may be posted for the protection of persons or property threatened with violence. Under such circumstances, coolness and firmness are the first requisites. No danger or circumstances will justify a sentinel in leaving his post without orders.

91. If a sentinel, from any cause, wishes to leave his post, he calls for the corporal of the guard, who

will relieve him, if necessary, by another sentinel, or take charge of his post until he can return to it. The following Articles of War show the importance with which a sentinel's post is invested.

"ART. 45. Any commissioned officer who shall be found drunk on his guard, party, or other duty, shall be cashiered. Any non-commissioned officer or soldier so offending shall suffer such corporeal punishment as shall be inflicted by the sentence of a court-martial.

"ART. 46. Any sentinel who shall be found sleeping upon his post, or shall leave it before he shall be regularly relieved, shall suffer death, or such other punishment as shall be inflicted by the sentence of a court-martial.

"ART. 50. Any officer or soldier who shall, without urgent necessity, or without the leave of his superior officer, quit his guard, platoon, or division, shall be punished, according to the nature of his offence, by the sentence of a court-martial."

92. There are instances where sentinels would seem almost justified in leaving their posts, as when their own lives are endangered by remaining, and there is no possibility of their affording the protection and guard for which they were posted, as when a camp or fort is shelled from a distance. Under such circumstances, if not relieved at once, call for the corporal of the guard.

93. When sentinels are required to remain at their posts at all hazards, the soldier has no alternative except to die at his post if necessary. No nobler death can fall to the lot of a soldier; whilst no greater ignominy can befall him than to desert his

post in time of danger, when the lives of others are dependent upon the performance of his duty.

94. To be surprised, or to fall asleep, in times of danger, is a crime of the gravest character, and punishable with death. Sometimes, when popular violence is threatened, the courage and firmness of a single sentinel may intimidate and keep back a mob, whilst timidity and doubt might encourage them. True courage will defend the post to the last. No man can desire a nobler death than to die in the cause of *right*.

95. Soldiers should know, however, that they are held responsible for the execution of their orders as well as their obedience; and they should, therefore, fully understand them. Ignorant and inexperienced officers sometimes give illegal and unjustifiable orders, for which the officer who gives them, and the soldier who obeys, may both be held responsible, either by military courts, or civil tribunals if there are any.

96. Soldiers should bear in mind that no orders will protect them in the commission of personal wrongs. They stand upon the same footing as any officer or citizen in civil life; and if a soldier, in the discharge of his orders, shoots a person, he may be arraigned and tried, and is at the mercy of a military court or jury, even when it is apparent that he will or should be acquitted. These are trying circumstances, and, fortunately, of rare occurrence;

but even these should not deter a soldier from doing what he knows and believes to be his duty.

97. Again, a sentinel, in the execution of his orders, has frequently the power to subject persons to great inconvenience and humiliation, who, from inadvertence or misapprehension, have come under his control. Whilst he might be sustained in the severity of his course, it is not contemplated that he shall abuse his authority or misuse his temporary power.

98. STABLE GUARD.—In cavalry and artillery, this guard is usually placed over the horses at night, to watch them and prevent any of them from making their escape or injuring themselves. It consists usually of a non-commissioned officer, and three men for each company or battery, and forms a separate detail. (Reg. 562.)

99. They may be put on with or without arms; and, although the same precision and attention as on camp guard are not required, they are equally responsible with other guards with regard to sleeping on post, or leaving or neglecting their duty in any way.

100. Neatness and correct soldierly bearing are enjoined on all sentinels. Precision in the compliments to officers, and in marching on and off duty, reflects credit upon the soldier, and secures to him the consideration and attention of his superiors.

101. Orderlies and color-sentinels are usually selected from the neatest, cleanest, and most soldierly-

looking member of the guard. These duties are of a lighter and more complimentary character, and are the first steps to promotion.

102. FATIGUE.—This term is applied to all duties not strictly military, such as laboring in the trenches, making roads, foraging, improving the grounds about a post or camp, &c., and is usually performed without arms, except when, in the vicinity of the enemy, it is necessary to guard against attack.

103. Fatigue-parties are always under the direction of an officer or non-commissioned officer, who is held responsible for the conduct of the men.

104. No soldier can leave his fatigue or working party, without permission from his superior officer, until he is regularly relieved.

105. Usually, in established camps and garrisons, the guard which marches off in the morning goes on fatigue the next morning, called "general police," for the purpose of sweeping and cleaning the common parade-ground, the vicinity of officers' quarters, and other places not immediately occupied by companies or detachments.

106. This detail, being consecutive with the guard, requires no other notification except the order that such will be the practice. Absentees from sickness and other causes are, therefore, not replaced, but must be accounted for.

107. In cases of more than ordinary fatigue or exposure, it is the custom to make an issue of whiskey to the men on fatigue. To obtain this issue,

the sergeant or corporal of police makes out a return, called an "extra return," giving the number of men and number of gills, one gill being allowed to each man. This return is signed by the officer in charge of the party; and it is then submitted to the commanding officer of the regiment, post, or detachment, who attaches his order for the issue, and the whiskey is then drawn from the commissary and issued to the men by the sergeant.

108. DAILY DUTY.—A soldier is on *daily duty* when he is put upon some continuous duty that excuses him from the ordinary company duty but does not entitle him to additional pay from the government,—such as company cooks, tailors, clerks, standing orderlies, &c. These duties may be performed by soldiers selected on account of special capacity or merit, or detailed in turn, as is most convenient and conducive to the interest of the service.

109. The *company cooks* are one or more men in each company detailed to do the cooking for the entire company. This is the case usually in companies where it is not the custom to distribute the provisions to the men; for in this case the messes furnish their own cooks, and they are not excused from any duty except what is absolutely necessary and which their messmates can do for them.

110. The law authorizes the detailing of one cook to thirty men, or less; two cooks if there are more than thirty men in the company. It also allows

to each cook two assistant cooks (colored), who are enlisted for the purpose, and are allowed ten dollars per month. (See par. 269.)

111. The cooks are under the direction of the first sergeant or commissary-sergeant, who superintends the issue of provisions and directs the cooking for each day. Company cooks for the whole company are generally detailed in turn, and for periods of a week or ten days.

112. *Company tailors.*—One or two tailors are usually detailed on daily duty in each company to fit and repair clothing for the men of the company. They are generally excused from such duties as materially interfere with their work, and receive such compensation from the men as will remunerate them for the materials they require and the extra work they may perform. This is usually done under the direction of the commanding officer of the company, under such regulations as he may establish.

113. *Company clerks.*—These are experienced penmen selected from the companies to assist the first sergeants in making out their returns, reports, muster-rolls, copying orders, &c. One to each company is generally sufficient to do all the writing, who are usually excused from such duties as the necessities of the service will justify.

114. *Orderlies* are soldiers selected on account of their intelligence, experience, and soldierly bearing, to attend on generals, commanding officers,

officers of the day, and staff officers, to carry orders, messages, &c. They may be taken from the guard daily, or put on permanently while the duty lasts: in the latter case they are reported on daily duty and are excused from all other duty that would interfere with their duty as orderlies.

115. EXTRA DUTY.—Where soldiers are detailed on some continuous duty or labor for ten days or longer, in the quartermaster, commissary, or some other department, where they are entitled to additional pay, it is called *"extra duty."* They are most generally employed in the quartermaster's department as mechanics, laborers, teamsters, &c., and are under the orders of, and paid by, the department in which they are employed.

116. They are generally excused from all military duty, except Sunday inspections, reviews, and musters, but may be required to attend drills when their instruction is not complete. Extra duty pay has been discontinued by the Act of March 3, 1863, sec. 35, but is still allowed in some cases, according to a decision of the Third Auditor.

117. DETACHED SERVICE.—When soldiers are sent away from their companies, under orders to do duty elsewhere, from the post, camp, or garrison, they are on *"detached service,"* and are so accounted for. The first for guard are detailed for detached service, and, if employed otherwise at the time, are relieved, if possible, in time to reach the camp or post to march with the detachment. This is

intended only for short and frequent detachments. In cases where the detachment is more or less permanent, it is not the custom to follow these rules, but to be guided, in making the details, by the nature of the service.

118. Where there is a possibility that the soldier may be detached for a long period, he should be accompanied by his descriptive roll and clothing-account, in order that he may draw his pay, and such clothing as he may need during his absence. This matter is sometimes overlooked by the officers, and should be remembered by the soldier, as he is most affected by the neglect.

DUTIES IN THE FIELD.

119. A soldier's duties in the field are nothing more than the practical application of the duties he has learned in camp or garrison to the purposes of war. Troops are said to be *"in the field"* when they are operating against the enemy, and are occupying temporarily the country, towns, cities, or entrenchments in the vicinity of the foe, or permanently encamped in their neighborhood. They are also said to be in the field when on the march through the country in times of peace.

120. In the field there are, in addition to camp-guards and police-guards, advanced guards, outposts, pickets, and reconnoissances. On these

guards the soldier's duty has not so much detail about it: much of the ceremony of camp-guard is omitted and modified to suit the circumstances; every thing is made subservient to the all-important end,—watching the enemy. His presence of mind, good judgment, and courage on these duties are put to the greatest test.

121. ADVANCED GUARDS are guards thrown out to the front in the direction in which the enemy is expected, to guard against attack or surprise. They may be composed of details united from the brigades, forming a "division-guard," and covering the front of the division, uniting with the guards of the divisions on the right and left; or "brigade-guards," composed of details from the different regiments of the brigade, and covering its front in the same manner.

122. The senior colonel or other officer of a "division-guard" is the "general officer of the day;" of a "brigade-guard," a field officer or senior captain is usually detailed as "field officer of the day." These guards are usually thrown some distance in the advance, sometimes several miles, and always far enough to give the troops time to form and prepare for battle before the enemy can come upon them. If the guards are thrown out too far to be relieved daily, they go on for several days at a time.

123. OUTPOSTS are isolated advanced guards of greater or less strength. When composed of small detachments, they are called "picket-guards."

124. RECONNOISSANCES are made by troops against the enemy for the purpose of finding out his position and strength. The term generally implies a strong party. When the force is small, it is more generally called "reconnoitring" or "scouting."

125. The special duty of the soldier in advanced guards, outposts, pickets, and reconnoissances, is that of *"picket," "skirmisher,"* and *"flanker."*

126. PICKET.—This term is used differently, and has different meanings in various works. It is used in our army to designate the advanced *sentinels* of an *"advanced guard."* Courage and common sense are the principal requisites for a *picket*.

127. The instructions which he receives are generally plain and easily understood: the only difficulty is to remember them at the critical moment. Pickets are either infantry or cavalry, or both together. The term *"vedette"* is frequently applied to cavalry pickets. The general rules for *picket* should be well understood by every soldier.

128. "The duties of the pickets are to keep a vigilant watch over the country in front, and over the movements of the enemy, if in sight, to prevent all unauthorized persons from passing in or out of the lines, and to arrest all suspicious individuals. In case of an attack, they will act as a line of skirmishers, and hold their ground to the last moment. If forced to retire, they will slowly close their intervals and fall back upon their supports." (General

Order No. 69, Head-Quarters Army of Potomac, 1862.) The following Regulations are important:—

"620. The sentinels and vedettes are placed on points from which they can see farthest, taking care not to break their connection with each other or with their posts. They are concealed from the enemy as much as possible by walls, or trees, or elevated ground. It is generally even of more advantage not to be seen than to see far. They should not be placed near covers, where the enemy may capture them.

"621. A sentinel should always be ready to fire; vedettes carry their pistols or carbines in their hands. A sentinel must be sure of the presence of an enemy before he fires; once satisfied of that, he must fire, though all defence on his part is useless, as the safety of the post may depend on it. Sentinels fire on all persons deserting to the enemy.

"622. If the post must be where a sentinel on it cannot communicate with the guard, a corporal and three men are detached for it, or the sentinels are doubled, that one may communicate with the guard. During the day the communication may be made by signals, such as raising a cap or handkerchief. At night sentinels are placed on low ground, the better to see objects against the sky.

"624. On the approach of any one at night, the sentinel orders—'*Halt!*' If the order is not obeyed after once repeated, he fires. If obeyed, he calls—'*Who goes there?*' If answered—'*Rounds*' or '*Patrol,*' he says—'*Stand: Advance one with the countersign.*' If more than one advance at the same time, or the person who advances fails to give the countersign or signal agreed on, the sentinel fires, and falls back to his guard. The sentinel over the arms, as soon as his hail is answered, turns out the guard, and the corporal goes to reconnoitre. When it is desirable to hide the position of the sentinel from the enemy, the hail is replaced by signals; the sentinel gives the signal, and those approaching the counter-signal.

"639. Bearers of flags are not permitted to pass the outer chain of sentinels; their faces are turned from the post or army; if necessary, their eyes are bandaged; a non-commissioned officer stays with them to prevent indiscretion of the sentinels.

"640. The commandant of the grand guard receipts for dispatches, and sends them to the field officer of the day or general of brigade, and dismisses the bearer; but if he has discovered what ought to be concealed from the enemy, he is detained as long as necessary.

"641. Deserters are disarmed at the advanced posts, and sent to the commander of the grand guard, who gets from them all the information he can concerning his post. If many come at night, they are received *cautiously, a few at a time.* They are sent in the morning to the field officer of the day, or to the nearest post or camp, to be conducted to the general of the brigade. All suspected persons are searched by the commanders of the posts."

129. Pickets should look out particularly for deserters; and parties representing themselves as such should be required to lay down their arms before they approach. A flag of truce should also be received with caution: it is usually a white flag, borne by an officer and accompanied by an escort. The flag is sometimes, particularly in the night, preceded by a trumpeter blowing the *parley.*

130. The escort is halted at a distance, and no one is permitted to advance except the bearer of

the flag. If the bearer has only a letter to deliver, it is taken and receipted for, and the bearer and his escort turned back to their own lines. If it is necessary to take the bearer to the commanding officer, his eyes are bandaged, and he is escorted thither.

131. Great precaution must be exercised with regard to parties passing out, to see that they are authorized to go and that they are not deserters. Soldiers frequently, from idle curiosity, or a spirit of adventure, or a desire for plunder, may take advantage of a friend or messmate being on post, and seek the indulgence of passing beyond the lines. Sentinels and soldiers should know that this is exceedingly irregular, and may be fraught with terrible consequences. No personal considerations should influence a soldier to so serious a neglect of his duty.

132. All sentinels of advanced guards should receive the countersign before sunset, and, whether this is neglected or not, they should commence challenging immediately after. Compliments are dispensed with on picket-duty.

133. The practice of pickets firing upon those of the enemy is barbarous; and retaliation is scarcely a sufficient excuse for doing it. Pickets should not fire unless an advance is intended, or in the cases heretofore indicated.

134. Firing on pickets has a tendency to produce false alarms, or its habitual practice may create indifference, and thus an actual attack pass unob-

served until a decided advantage is gained by the enemy.

135. The habit of pickets communicating with those of the enemy is irregular, and should not be indulged in, unless sometimes by the officers for some specific object.

136. SKIRMISHERS are soldiers thrown forward and deployed at intervals of from ten to twenty paces, according to the point they are to cover; if a column on the march, or a line of battle advancing to attack, to conceal the movements or to give timely notice of the enemy. They may be either infantry or cavalry.

137. On the march, the column usually proceeds on the road, preceded by an advanced guard proportioned to the strength of the column,—usually about one-tenth of the whole force. From this the skirmishers are taken, one-third being retained for a reserve; the remainder are deployed as skirmishers on the right and left of the road, and from one hundred and fifty to three hundred yards in advance of the reserve, which itself is about four hundred yards in advance of the head of the column.

138. A non-commissioned officer, with two or three men, march on the road, and the skirmishers, on the right and left of the road, regulate their march on them. In this manner the march is conducted under the direction of the commanding officer of the advance, who has his instructions from the commander of the column.

139. The skirmishers should endeavor not to advance beyond or fall in rear of the line, should keep their proper intervals, and be guided by the centre of the line.

140. Skirmishers should use their eyes and ears. They are the feelers with which the army searches its way into the enemy's country; and every suspicious or important circumstance should be reported at once to their immediate superiors. No one should be allowed to escape from their approach who might give information to the enemy; and all suspicious characters should be arrested and sent to the rear.

141. When skirmishers precede a line of battle preliminary to an attack, they advance and engage the enemy, unless otherwise instructed; and when the line arrives within range of the enemy, they are usually recalled, and form in the rear of the command to which they belong.

142. FLANKERS are skirmishers placed on the flanks of an advancing column, three or four hundred yards distant, extending from the extremities of the line of skirmishers to the rear of the column, and parallel to it. They march in file, with intervals of ten to twenty paces.

143. Their duty is to guard against an attack from the flank, and to give notice of the approach of an enemy in that direction. Their duties are entirely similar to those of skirmishers; and when forced to retire, they fall back fighting, and form on

their reserves or supports that are marching inside of them in the direction of the column.

THE INFANTRY SOLDIER.

144. In the infantry is the main strength of an army. Cavalry and artillery are the auxiliaries. The final results of a war or campaign are achieved by this arm of the service; and the foot-soldier should bear in mind the importance of his position, and seek to achieve the highest perfection of his arm. No cavalry or artillery can stand against perfect infantry properly handled.

145. The sharpshooters, deployed as skirmishers, and supported by the main column of infantry, out of range, will pick off the cannoneers, and silence in a short time a battery of artillery; and the best cavalry will disperse before a line of infantry that reserves its fire until the enemy is within short range, and show a determination to receive them on the bayonets of their empty muskets.

146. The infantry soldier should bear in mind that, with whatever exultation the cavalry or artillery pass him in advancing upon the enemy, the grand result cannot be achieved without him, and that the presence of the musket and its proximity is what enables them to precede him in the fight.

147. A well-instructed and disciplined infantry-

man is always prepared for duty. His hours of leisure are devoted to preparation. His clothing is prepared and cleaned, his knapsack always packed, his arms and accoutrements in order, and his ammunition secure.

148. The supply of necessary articles in the field should be limited to the smallest possible amount; and industry will make up for many a deficient article. Messes unite, and each carries an article that can be used in common.

149. By repeated washings and cleanings, one suit of clothes can be made to look as well as if a change were on hand. For fatigue-duties, thin cotton overalls and blouse worn over the only suit will protect it and make it last much longer, and are much lighter than an extra suit.

150. The shoes are the most important item of clothing to the foot-soldier. The army bootee is much the best. The soles should be broad, the heels low and broad. Woollen socks should be worn. The feet should be bathed frequently in cold water. Boots are universally impracticable for marching. If the ankles require support, the French gaiter can be worn: they are also a very good protection from the mud and dust, and protect the trousers.

151. An hour's drill, morning and afternoon, when not marching, is a necessary exercise, no matter what may be the proficiency of the regiment or company. It keeps the body in condition for service at any moment, and is conducive to health.

152. A good soldier makes his company and regiment his home, and never absents himself without proper permission, and then returns punctually at the expiration of his pass. The habit of always being absent is exceedingly pernicious; it cultivates tastes and habits that are detrimental to the soldier's best interest, and he is almost sure to be absent when most wanted, and loses, perhaps, a favorable moment to do himself a credit.

153. He should learn to wait: a soldier's life is made up in waiting for the critical moments. The times in distinction are few, and quickly pass; and, once gone, he has a long time to wait for the next opportunity. Constant training and faithful watching are necessary, so that he may see the proper moment and be in the best possible condition to perform his duty.

154. A soldier is dependent on his officers for pay, clothing, subsistence, and medical attendance; but his health, success, and promotion depend, in the main, upon himself. Within certain limits, he must look out for himself.

155. He must learn to make the most of his pay and allowances. His rations are abundant for his subsistence, and, if not always palatable, a little ingenuity in cooking, a little management in exchanging for the products of the country, will make his rations do him; whilst spending his pay for things to eat, and disregarding his rations, is a want of frugality that should be corrected.

156. His clothing is also sufficient; and many soldiers save from sixty to one hundred dollars of their clothing allowance, which is paid to them in money at the expiration of their enlistment. A little industry in mending and cleaning his clothes will well reward his labors in the savings of the frugal soldier. To this end, he should be provided with a little wallet, containing an assortment of thread, needles, buttons, scissors, &c., and should economize and use up faithfully his allowance of soap.

157. He can readily save all his pay, and make his spending-money by labor during leisure hours in many ways which are afforded him in the vicinity of a camp or garrison. The effort, however, to lay up money should not be carried to an extent that would interfere with his duties as a soldier.

THE CAVALRY SOLDIER.

158. THE cavalry soldier is apt to look with some contempt as he rides by the weary footman carrying his knapsack; but he should bear in mind how much he is dependent upon him, and how much of the confidence with which he rides to the front is due to the staunch columns of infantry he leaves in his rear, and how soon he may be compelled to

seek refuge from the enemy's sharpshooters and artillery in the rear of the same columns of infantry.

159. A cavalry solider should not exceed in weight one hundred and sixty pounds, should be active and strong, physically sound, with a natural fondness for horses and experience in handling them. His duties are more arduous and severe than those of the footman. His first care should be his horse at all times. The two are inseparable, and one is of little account without the other. A dismounted cavalry soldier, leading a broken-down horse and trudging wearily along in the rear of the column, is a pitiable and ridiculous sight; whilst the perfect cavalry soldier, neatly dressed, arms and accoutrements in perfect order, his horse well fed and thoroughly groomed, and riding with ease, grace, and self-possession, is always an object of admiration.

160. The general duties of the cavalry soldier are the same as those of the infantry soldier, varying only on account of his horse and the difference in the character of the service.

161. Great care and attention are necessary to keep the horse in condition for service. The following hints are offered:—

The horse should always be used moderately, having much additional weight to carry. The habitual gait of cavalry is a walk, and it should not be increased, unless necessary or acting under orders.

162. Horses should never be watered or fed when heated, nor should they be used violently immediately after watering or feeding. Heating food, such as corn or wheat, should not be fed in large quantities at a time, but divided into two or more feeds; and this is particularly necessary when hay or grass is scarce. They should be fed salt two or three times a week.

163. The horse should be carefully groomed. When heated, in cold or chilly weather, particularly in the open air, if required to stand still, he should have a blanket thrown over him until he is cool; nor should he be washed or drenched with water, except when cool. If covered with mud, it is better to let it remain until the horse is dry, and then let him be groomed as soon as he is dry: it should not be permitted to remain any longer than necessary. If the mud is rubbed off when wet, it causes the sand to be rubbed into the skin, and is much more difficult to remove afterwards.

164. The back should always be examined after riding. Any evidence of soreness should be arrested by a judicious folding of blanket and care in adjusting the saddle, by shortening or lengthening the crupper. Any swelling or scalding from the saddle should be frequently washed in cold water, to check inflammation.

165. When halting on the march, horses have a disposition to roll, that frequently injures the saddle and accoutrements. This may be in a great

measure prevented by removing the saddle and rubbing the horse's back with currycomb, brush, or a whisp of straw or twigs. During such halts, every opportunity to let the horse graze a little, or feeding him on a handful of hay or grass, or other feed, gathered by the way, should not be neglected: the horse's stomach is small in proportion to his size, and such care of him will keep him in good condition where without it he would break down.

166. When a horse gets sick, the veterinary surgeon should at once be consulted. Soldiers are not permitted to prescribe for their horses without permission from their company commanders.

167. The horse has been found to be demoralizing to the habits of the soldier. The cavalry service removes the cavalry-man more from the immediate control of his officers; he is enabled soon to become more familiar with the surrounding country, on his duties as messenger, orderly, foraging, reconnoitring, picket and outpost duty, his temptations to straggle and commit depredations are much greater, the chances of detection are less, and the violation of orders is attended with much less personal fatigue and inconvenience; and hence the irregularities peculiar to the cavalry service.

168. Cavalry-men, however, should bear in mind that these facilities are no excuse for misdemeanors of irregularities; and every soldier should have the interest of his own corps too much at heart to aid or abet in misconduct that gives to his arm of service

such a disagreeable notoriety. He should labor to give his own corps as high a reputation for good conduct as the foot-soldier. He should not allow himself to be excelled in propriety by the infantry-man.

169. The arms and accoutrements of cavalry, being more numerous and subject to more wear and tear, require more labor and attention than those of infantry, but should not for that reason be any more neglected. This care is equally important, and the beneficial results of cleanliness and order are quite as satisfactory, as in any other arm.

170. Every article that is issued to the man has its use and importance. The articles should be frequently overhauled, and kept in repair. The sabre should be kept sharp, the arms clean and in order, the ammunition close and compact, to prevent rubbing, and secure against moisture. The straps should be kept repaired, well cleaned and oiled. The nose-bag and lariat-rope are not sufficiently appreciated. The health of the horse is dependent upon his being taught to eat his feed from the nose-bag, as feeding from the ground causes the horse to take up with his food great quantities of gravel and sand, thereby injuring his digestion. The lariat-rope is important for the purpose of forage—either for the transportation of forage, or picketing the horse out at night to enable him to graze, the opportunity for which should never be neglected.

171. An important article is a forage-bag, made

like a saddle-bag with a slit in it. It should be at
least a yard long and a foot wide, in which to carry
one or two feeds, so that accident or delay will not
deprive the horse of his regular feed. It can be
readily made by any soldier out of an ordinary
grain-sack.

THE ARTILLERY SOLDIER.

172. IN our service, Artillery is divided into *Artillery Proper*, *Light Artillery*, and *Heavy Artillery*.

173. ARTILLERY PROPER, sometimes called FOOT
ARTILLERY, or FIELD ARTILLERY, is divided into batteries, manned by one company, and provided with
four, six, or eight guns, according to the strength of
the company.

174. The battery is divided into sections, two
pieces making a section, commanded by the lieutenants, or, in their absence, by the ranking sergeants. The sergeants are usually assigned to the
different guns, and are called Chiefs of Piece. The
gunners are usually taken from the corporals.

175. The men, except the drivers and chiefs of
piece, are dismounted, and ride on the caissons and
limbers, or march in order by the side of the carriages. They are sometimes armed with pistols or
cutlasses, or both.

176. LIGHT ARTILLERY, sometimes called HORSE ARTILLERY, is similar to foot artillery, except that all the men are mounted, thus uniting the duties of cavalry with artillery.

177. HEAVY ARTILLERY is generally used for garrisoning forts and intrenched places, where the armament is composed of guns of greater caliber than field-pieces. In the field, they generally have charge of the siege-train. The troops are usually armed, equipped, and drilled as infantry, in addition to their duties with the large guns.

178. The artillery soldier is expected to be more or less familiar with all the duties expected of cavalry and infantry, as in field-batteries they have a similar care of horses, and in heavy artillery they are required to perform all the duties required of infantry, at times. He is required to know all about guard-duties. They are not, however, required to do as much outpost, fatigue, or picket duty, and only in the absence of the proper troops for such duty.

179. The peculiarities with which an artillery soldier in a field-battery must familiarize himself, in addition to most of the duties of cavalry and infantry, is the care of guns and harness, and especially the ammunition. He should understand well the principles in firing, and peculiarities of the particular gun and the ammunition used in the battery.

180. During the firing, he must learn to be com-

posed, and guard against being confused by the
noise of the cannon and the commotion among the
horses. He must use his eyes, as well as his ears,
and watch his own piece and the workings of his
companions.

181. Where pieces are massed close together, he
is apt to mistake the firing of an adjoining piece for
his own; and many a man has been killed or injured
by jumping in at the command "load" at an adjoining piece, just as his own gunner gave the command "fire." To prevent the hearing from being
injured by the concussion, the ears may be pro-
tected by a little cotton. The shock is also lessened
by keeping the mouth open.

182. No. 3, who tends the vent, should be particularly careful to keep it closed and air-tight. This is
necessary whilst sponging, to assist in extinguish-
ing any remains of the cartridge that may be on fire
in the chamber, and whilst loading, to prevent the
fire from igniting the cartridge. He should not remove his thumb from the vent until every cannoneer is clear of the piece.

183. No. 4 should observe that every man is
clear of the piece before he fires.

184. No. 2 should observe that No. 3 has the vent
well closed when he inserts the cartridge. He
should be careful to insert the cartridge correctly.
The bottom should go in first, and the seam on the
side.

185. No. 5 should keep the cartridge in the ammunition-pouch until he delivers it to No. 2.

186. The gunner and the chief of piece should attend closely and see that the cannoneers do not neglect any of the above instructions, and the men at the limber and caissons should keep the boxes open as little as possible. Each cannoneer should be familiar with all the duties of each post, so that they may be replaced.

187. All the cannoneers should be perfectly familiar with all the different kinds of ammunition, their uses and application, and where they are to be found. They should understand the uses of the implements in the ammunition-chest; how to spike a gun, and how to remove a spike; how to blow up ammunition-chests, and render artillery unserviceable temporarily and permanently. The greater the extent to which the solider carries this kind of knowledge, in addition to his other duties, the more serviceable will he be, and the greater will be his chances for promotion.

188. HEAVY ARTILLERY, in addition to knowledge of the ammunition and implements of gunnery, requires a practical knowledge of the forces and appliances for handling and moving heavy guns. This kind of information is not easily acquired from books; and, moreover, the appliances that may be available at one time may not be on hand at another; and tact for applying make-shifts is an essential qualification.

189. The companies are divided into detachments, whose strength is dependent upon the kind of guns used, and the detachments are officered in proportion. The same general principles and commands are used, although varying a little, as the carriage and implements of different kinds of guns vary.

The principal books of instruction for artillery are "Gibbon's Manual," "Manual for Heavy Artillery," prepared by a Board of Officers, and "Anderson's Field Artillery." An excellent little book for instruction is "Roberts's Handbook of Artillery."

THE ORDNANCE SOLDIER.

190. ENLISTED men of ordnance are not so much soldiers as mechanics and laborers. They are employed in arsenals and armories for the manufacture and care of ordnance. They are enlisted like other men, but differently employed, and receive different allowances of pay, clothing, and rations.

191. Master armorers, master carriage-makers, master blacksmiths, now called sergeants of ordnance, receive thirty-four dollars per month. Armorers, carriage-makers, and blacksmiths, now called corporals, receive twenty dollars per month. Artificers, now called privates of the first class, receive eighteen dollars per month; and laborers,

now called privates of the second class, receive sixteen dollars per month.

192. Sergeants and corporals receive a ration and a half per day, and the privates one ration. The sergeants are not entitled to an allowance for clothing; whilst the corporals and privates receive the same clothing as other enlisted men of the line.

193. The appointments of sergeants must be submitted to the Chief of Ordnance for his approval (Regulation 1445); but corporals and privates are mustered according to their competency, at the discretion of the officer in command. All enlisted men of ordnance enlist as privates of the lowest class, and are advanced subsequently according to their competency, and may be reduced, at the discretion of the officer in command, except the sergeants, whose reduction must be approved by the Chief of Ordnance the same as their appointment.

194. Ordnance sergeants for posts are enlisted differently and intended for different duty. (See Ordnance Sergeant, Par. 246.)

195. The enlisted men are under the direction of the commanding officers of the arsenal or armory, and the master workman, and are subject to such rules and regulations as are prescribed by the commanding officer and approved by the Chief of Ordnance, and published to the men.

196. Ordnance soldiers are paid by military storekeepers appointed to disburse the funds appropriated to the Ordnance Department.

THE ENGINEER SOLDIER.

197. ENGINEER soldiers are enlisted like other soldiers, and are similarly organized and instructed. They receive, however, different pay, and, as a class, are expected to be superior men. Recruiting officers are directed to make more rigid examination and to give preference to the best mechanics and educated men. At present there are only five companies of engineer soldiers in the United States service.

198. The pay of engineer soldiers is as follows:— sergeants, thirty-four dollars per month; corporals, twenty dollars per month; privates of the first class, eighteen dollars per month; privates of the second class, sixteen dollars per month. Rations and clothing are nearly the same as other troops.

199. They are expected to know all the garrison and field duties of soldiers of the line, and, in addition, the practical duties involved in the construction of fortifications, bridges, &c. For this reason, mechanics and educated men are preferred; and their promotion to privates of the first class, and to non-commissioned officers, depends upon their superior intelligence and progress in every department of practical military knowledge.

SIGNAL CORPS.

200. THE law allows in this corps the enlistment of one sergeant, two privates of the first class, and four of the second class, with pay, clothing, and rations of engineers, to each signal officer. Each army corps or department is allowed from six to eight signal officers: the number of officers and enlisted men is, therefore, limited by the number of departments or army corps. (Act March 3, 1863, section 17.)

201. The men are enlisted and re-enlisted the same as other soldiers, and the same high standard that is required for the engineer corps is demanded for this service. Recruiting officers for the signal corps are instructed to be very rigid in their examination of recruits. Enlisted men of other arms may be transferred to it, with the consent of commanding officers of regiments. Applications are made in the same manner as for any other transfer. The soldier must, however, submit to an examination before he will be accepted.

202. The men are mounted, armed, and equipped as light cavalry, and the uniform is the same. No drill has been specified for them except the manipulation of the signals, in which they are instructed by the officers. They should, however, understand the use of their arms, ride well, and understand the care of horses. They should also understand all the duties of their grade in the line, and be true soldiers in all respects.

203. They are sworn to secrecy, and prohibited from communicating any information they may become possessed of or acquire in the course of their duty or instruction. They should be active, athletic young men, of medium size; quick, intelligent, with superior eyesight; of good judgment and undoubted courage. They should have at least a good common-school education, and be able to write well.

204. Their duty is very similar to that of mounted patrol duty, and they usually accompany the advance of an army or body of troops sent out for observation. They are not called upon to fight, except in self-defense,—which may be frequently necessary, owing to their exposed position. At such times they should be prepared to destroy their signals, instruments, and papers when capture seems inevitable, to prevent their falling into the hands of the enemy. They are frequently exposed to the perils of scouts and reconnoitring parties, and should, therefore, be always in uniform, unless they are willing to run the risk of being apprehended and punished as spies.

SPECIAL ENLISTMENTS.

205. THERE are a number of special appointments or positions, for which men are enlisted in

the service, that differ in their duties from those of soldiers of the line, viz.:—

Veterinary Surgeon.
Medical Cadet.
Drum-Major, Principal or Chief Musician, Chief Trumpeter, Trumpeter.
Musician.
Saddler Sergeant and Saddler.
Ordnance Sergeant.
Hospital Steward.
Farrier, Blacksmith, and Artificer.
Wagoner.
African Under-Cook.

206. When men are enlisted for any of the above positions, and mustered into service as such, they cannot be reduced to private soldiers. If they have been enlisted as soldiers and promoted to these positions, they may by sentence of court-martial be reduced.

207. Men enlisted as above, although subject to the Rules and Articles of War, and to obedience to orders and regulations, cannot be assigned to other than their legitimate duties, except in cases of manifest necessity, or when unemployed at their legitimate duties for necessary reasons. Some are part of the legal organization of regiments, whilst others exist only by special enactment of Congress. A brief summary of their duties will be given.

208. VETERINARY SURGEON.—By sec. 37, Act March 3, 1863, one veterinary surgeon is allowed to

each cavalry regiment, instead of a chief farrier, with the rank of sergeant-major and a compensation of seventy-five dollars per month. The implication by the law is that he shall be enlisted into service as other soldiers although it is not so stated.

209. General Order No. 259, 1863, provides that he shall be selected by a board of three regimental officers next in rank to the commanding officer, and his name transmitted to the Chief of the Cavalry Bureau, and by him submitted to the Secretary of War for appointment. A record of all the appointments is kept in the Adjutant-General's Office.

210. It would seem, therefore, that he is not to be regarded as an enlisted man, but has all the privileges of an appointment, and can therefore resign his position on the approval of the appointing power. His resignation would therefore be acted on in the same manner as that of an officer. There is, however, very little legislation upon his duties; he is allowed seventy-five dollars per month, but there is no provision for rations, or any other allowances.

211. His duties are implied to be the care and cure of sick and disabled horses in his regiment. A considerable education is therefore requisite, involving a knowledge of the anatomy and physiology of the horse, a knowledge of chemistry sufficient to understand the character and use of the chemicals and medicines used in the treatment of horses, besides a practical knowledge and experience in the diseases to which horses are subject.

212. His duties also involve the charge of the horse-medicines allowed. These are furnished by the Quartermaster's Department. He must, therefore, obtain them from the regimental quartermaster, to whom he renders an account of this expenditure, as they are accounted for on his property return, with other quartermaster's property.

213. MEDICAL CADETS.—Seventy Medical Cadets are allowed by law to the medical staff of the army. Their pay is thirty dollars per month, and one ration. They enlist for one year, and are subject to the Rules and Articles of War, and their rank and pay is the same as that of the Military Cadet at West Point. (See Act August 3, 1861, section 5, and April 16, 1862, section 1.)

214. They are required to be young men of liberal education, students of medicine, between the ages of eighteen and twenty-three, who have been reading medicine for two years, and have attended at least one course of lectures in a medical college.

215. Their duties are to act as dressers in the general hospitals, and as ambulance attendants in the field, under the direction and control of the medical officers alone.

216. On the fifteenth day of the last month of their service, the near approach of their discharge shall be reported to the Surgeon-General, in order, if desired, that they may be relieved by another detail of applicants.

217. It would seem, in the absence of any pub-

lished regulations, that applicants for the Medical Cadet Corps should apply to the Surgeon-General at Washington, from whence they would be informed where to report for examination and enlistment.

218. DRUM-MAJOR.—For each of the new regiments of infantry, one drum-major or leader of the band is allowed, with the pay and emoluments of a second lieutenant of infantry. (Act July 29, 1861, section 4.)

219. The law with regard to drum-majors is obscure, as it allows in the same section only the pay of sergeant of cavalry, seventeen dollars; yet no drum-majors are allowed or recognized by law except in the infantry regiments of the new army, which by the same law provides that their pay shall be that of second lieutenant of infantry, implying, however, that the drum-major shall also be the leader of the band.

220. The duties of a drum-major are not prescribed by law or regulations, and are only deduced by custom. He performs the same duties with reference to the band that the first sergeant does in relation to the company. He parades the band at roll-call and calls the roll, superintends the police of their quarters, makes out the provision returns, and attends to the drawing of rations and other issues to the band.

221. He has the immediate care of the public property in use by the band. He is under the orders

and instructions of the adjutant of the regiment. He drills and instructs the band in their military duties; and the company musicians are usually under his charge and instruction.

222. As leader of the band, he would in addition have charge of the instruction of the musicians, the arranging of the music, and the selection.

223. PRINCIPAL MUSICIANS.—The law allows to each regiment of regular infantry, the Fifth Artillery, and to each volunteer infantry regiment, two principal or chief musicians. Other laws with regard to bands make the position of chief musicians anomalous and inconsistent. (Act July 29, 1861.)

224. The Act of July 5, 1838, section 16, allows the chief musician seventeen dollars per month, whilst section 4, Act July 29, 1861, provides that bands shall be paid as follows: one-fourth of the twenty-four shall receive the pay of sergeants of engineers, thirty-four dollars, one-fourth the pay of corporals of engineers, twenty dollars, and one-half the pay of privates of engineers of the first class, seventeen dollars.

225. As the principal musicians are in addition to the foregoing, it follows that they get no more than the lowest class of musicians. The leader of the band, by the 4th section of the above Act, is entitled to the pay and emoluments of a second lieutenant of infantry: yet there are no leaders authorized, except in the nine new regiments of

infantry. It will be seen, therefore, that the foregoing laws are quite incongruous.

226. LEADER OF THE BAND.—Where there is no leader of the band authorized, as is the case in the old regiments of artillery and infantry, and in all the cavalry regiments, one of the principal musicians acts as the leader of the band. To secure a competent musician for this purpose, the leader usually receives additional pay out of the regimental fund, or by voluntary contribution from the regiment. Leaders of brigade and regimental bands now receive seventy-five dollars per month. (Act June 20, 1864.)

227. The leader of the band is charged with the instruction of the band and the selection and arrangement of the music. He is also charged, in the absence of a drum-major, with the duties usually assigned to him. Like the drum-major, he receives his orders and instructions from the adjutant of the regiment, or, as leader of a brigade band, from the adjutant-general of the brigade.

228. BANDS.—A band is allowed to some regiments by law, and provision is made for the payment of such; but the authority granted in the Regulations, to detail soldiers for a band for such regiments as are not thus provided for, authorizes only the application of the regimental fund for support of bands in addition to their salary as soldiers.

229. The law allows a band to each of the new regiments of artillery and infantry. The bands are

authorized to have not more than twenty-four musicians; and in the old regiments of infantry they are by the War Department limited to sixteen. The drum-majors and principal musicians are not included in this allowance for the band, nor are the company musicians. Cavalry regiments are not authorized to have bands.

230. The Act of June 20, 1864, fixes the pay of the principal musicians at twenty-two dollars per month, and of the other musicians at sixteen, but fails to state what proportion shall be principal musicians. The leaders in the bands of regular regiments, where no leader is authorized, usually are remunerated out of the regimental fund, or by contributions.

231. Each brigade of volunteers is allowed a band of sixteen musicians, and a leader at seventy-five dollars per month. The law is not clear as to whether the leader is one of the sixteen or in addition to them. These bands receive the same pay that the regular regiments do.

232. The cavalry regiments of the regular service, and all the regiments of the volunteer service, can have bands, under the authority granted in paragraph 81, Revised Regulations. Sixteen soldiers are detailed *pro rata* from the companies, and instructed in music. An additional pay may be allowed them out of the regimental fund.

233. They are, for the time-being, dropped from

the company returns and rolls, and are mustered on the staff roll. One of the principal musicians can be used as leader of the band, who is remunerated the same as the musicians.

234. MUSICIANS.—Each company of infantry, artillery, and engineers is allowed two musicians,—a drummer and a fifer; and in cavalry, two trumpeters. These are independent of the musicians allowed to the band. They are on the footing of privates with respect to pay, clothing, and rations. They are instructed by the drum-major or principal musician.

235. In the cavalry regiments the trumpeters are instructed by the chief trumpeter. There is no provision for an instructor of music in the four old artillery regiments. In batteries and companies of light artillery, the musicians are instructed as buglers. The companies of artillery equipped as infantry have, like infantry, a drummer and fifer.

236. Musicians of infantry, artillery, and engineers have no arms, except a musician's sword, issued to them. The trumpeters have sabres and pistols. They take charge of the instruments used by them, and are responsible for them. They are not put on the ordinary duty of soldiers, but are liable for fatigue duties and are used as orderlies.

237. They take their turns at the guard-house for sounding the calls. When the companies of

the regiment are together, the musicians of each company are united for the purpose of instruction and exercise. When a company, however, is detached, the musicians that belong to it go with it.

238. On the march, at drills or parades, all the musicians are united in a body. They draw their rations and mess with their companies. The principal musician or chief trumpeter keeps the roster and makes the details; and they are not under the first sergeant's orders, except when acting with the company.

239. One or two musicians march on with the guard, and remain with it at the guard-house during the tour, and sound the musicians' call ten minutes before the *Assembly*, at which signal all the musicians assemble. The roll is called by the chief musician, drum-major, or chief trumpeter, and then they all unite in sounding the calls for the companies.

240. It has been the practice of the service to enlist boys under eighteen as musicians and trumpeters for companies, where they show a musical capacity. The consent of the parent or guardian is necessary to legalize the enlistment. They are generally collected at depots, and instructed in music before they are assigned to regiments and companies. Boys are allowed the same pay, clothing, and rations as men in the same capacity.

241. CHIEF TRUMPETER.—The chief trumpeter in cavalry regiments occupies the corresponding posi-

tion to drum-major, or principal musician, in the other regiments. The trumpeters are instructed by him, and he is held responsible for their neatness and appearance on duty and their presence at roll-calls. His pay is that of chief bugler, twenty-three dollars per month.

242. He keeps the roster, and makes the details from the trumpeters for orderlies, guard, fatigue, and other duties.

243. SADDLER SERGEANT.—Each regiment of cavalry is allowed a saddler sergeant, with the pay and emoluments of a regimental commissary sergeant, seventeen dollars per month. His duties are not defined by law or regulation. He would naturally, however, have charge of the company saddlers of the regiment, and act as master saddler or foreman when the company saddlers are united in one shop for the repair of the equipments of the companies.

244. He takes his instructions from the commanding officer of the regiment, and should attend to the repairs of the horse-equipments of the field, staff, and band, and see that the company saddlers perform properly their duties in the companies.

245. SADDLERS.—Each company of cavalry is allowed an enlisted man as saddler, whose duty it is to keep the horse-equipments of the company in repair, under the direction of the company commander and the saddler sergeant. The pay of saddler is fourteen dollars per month, the same as

a corporal of cavalry, with the same allowance of clothing and rations. Military duty ordinarily is not required of either saddler sergeants or saddlers; but they should be instructed in a knowledge of the ordinary duties, and should at all times be available in case of necessity.

246. ORDNANCE SERGEANT.—Each military post may have an ordnance sergeant, whose duty it is to take charge of all the surplus ordnance at the post. He is enlisted for the position and belongs to the post, and is not removed when the troops are changed. His pay is twenty-two dollars per month, one ration, and allowance for clothing. Ordnance sergeants do not belong to the Ordnance Department, but to the non-commissioned staff, unattached, of the regiment or post.

247. The following are the Regulations governing the appointment and duties of ordnance sergeant:—

"131. The Secretary of War selects from the sergeants of the *line* of the army, who may have faithfully served eight years (four years in the grade of non-commissioned officer), as many ordnance sergeants as the service may require, not exceeding one to each military post.

"132. Captains will report to their colonels such sergeants as, by their conduct and service, merit such appointment, setting forth the description, length of service of the sergeant, the portion of his service he was a non-commissioned officer, his general character as to fidelity and sobriety, his qualifications as a clerk, and his fitness for the duties to be performed by an ordnance sergeant. These reports will be forwarded to the Adjutant-General, to be laid before the Secretary of War, with an application in the following form:—

HEAD-QUARTERS, ETC.

To the Adjutant-General:

Sir:—I forward, for consideration of the proper authority, an application for the appointment of Ordnance Sergeant.

Name and Regiment.	Letter of Company.	Length of Service.				Remarks.
		As non-commissioned Officer.		In the Army.		
		Years.	Months.	Years.	Months.	

Enclosed herewith you will receive the report of —, the officer commanding the company in which the sergeant has been serving, to which I add the following remarks:

—— —, Commanding—Regiment.

"133. When a company is detached from the headquarters of the regiment, the reports of the commanding officer in this matter will pass to the regimental headquarters through the commanding officer of the post or detachment, and be accompanied by his opinion as to the fitness of the candidate.

"134. Ordnance sergeants will be assigned to posts when appointed, and are not to be transferred to other stations, except by orders from the Adjutant-General's Office.

"135. At the expiration of their term of service, ordnance sergeants may be re-enlisted, provided they shall have conducted themselves in a becoming manner, and performed their duties to the satisfaction of the commanding officer. If the commanding officer, however, shall not think proper to re-enlist the ordnance sergeant of his post, he will communicate to the Adjutant-General his reasons for declining to re-enlist him, in time to receive the decision of the War Department before the sergeant may lawfully claim to re-enlist.

"136. The officers interested must be aware, from the nature of the duties assigned to ordnance sergeants, that the judicious selection of them is of no small importance to the interests of the service; and that while the law contemplates, in the appointment of these non-commissioned officers, the better preservation of the ordnance and ordnance stores in deposit in the several forts, there is the further motive of offering a reward to those faithful and well-tried sergeants who have long served their country, and of thus giving encouragement to the soldier in the ranks to emulate them in conduct, and thereby secure substantial promotion. Colonels and captains cannot, therefore, be too particular in investigating the characters of the candidates, and in giving their testimony as to their merits.

"137. The appointment and removal of ordnance sergeants, stationed at military posts, in pursuance of the above provisions of law, shall be reported by the Adjutant-General to the Chief of the Ordnance Department.

"138. When a non-commissioned officer receives the

appointment of ordnance sergeant, he shall be dropped from the rolls of the regiment or company in which he may be serving at the time.

"139. The duty of ordnance sergeants relates to the care of the ordnance, arms, ammunition and other military stores at the post to which they may be attached, under the direction of the commanding officer, and according to the regulations of the Ordnance Department.

"140. If a post be evacuated, the ordnance sergeant shall remain on duty at the station, under the direction of the Chief of the Ordnance Department, in charge of the ordnance and ordnance stores, and of such other public property as is not in charge of some officer or agent of other departments; for which ordnance stores and other property he will account to the chiefs of the proper departments until otherwise directed.

"141. An ordnance sergeant in charge of ordnance stores at a post where there is no commissioned officer shall be held responsible for the safe-keeping of the property, and he shall he governed by the regulations of the Ordnance Department in making issues of the same, and in preparing and furnishing the requisite returns. If the means at his disposal are not sufficient for the preservation of the property, he shall report the circumstances to the Chief of the Ordnance Department.

"142. Ordnance Sergeants are to be considered as belonging to the non-commissioned staff of the post, under the orders of the commanding officer. They are to wear the uniform of the Ordnance Department, with the distinctive badges prescribed for the non-commissioned staff of regiments of artillery; and they are to appear under arms with the troops at all reviews and inspections, monthly and weekly.

"143. When serving at any post which may be the head-quarters of a regiment, ordnance sergeants shall be reported by name on the post returns, and mustered with the non-commissioned staff of the regiment; and at all other posts they shall be mustered and reported in some company stationed at the post at which they serve; be paid on the muster-roll, and be charged with the clothing and all other supplies previously received from any officer, or subsequently issued to them by the commanding officer of the company for the time-being. Whenever the company may be ordered from the post, the ordnance sergeant will be transferred to the rolls of any remaining company, by the order of the commanding officer of the post.

"144. In the event of the troops being all withdrawn from a post at which there is an ordnance sergeant, he shall be furnished with his descriptive roll and account of clothing and pay, signed by the proper officer last in command, accompanied by the remarks necessary for his military history; and on his exhibiting such papers to any paymaster, with a letter from the Ordnance Office acknowledging the receipt of his returns, and that they are satisfactory, he will he paid on a separate account the amount which may be due him at the date of the receipt of the returns mentioned in such letter, together with commutation of rations, according to the regulations of the Subsistence Department. A certified statement of his pay account will be furnished the ordnance sergeant by the paymaster by whom he may be last paid. When there are no troops at the post, the ordnance sergeant will report to the Adjutant-General's Office, by letter, on the last day of every month."

248. The commanding officer is responsible for the ordnance stores, and the returns are signed by

him. The ordnance sergeant, therefore, takes his orders from him. When, however, there are no commissioned officer or troops at the post, he makes the returns in his own name.

249. By Regulation 140, an ordnance sergeant may also be placed in charge of property belonging to other departments, in the case of evacuation of the post by the troops, in which case he is required to make the prescribed returns, the same as an officer, to the department to which the property appertains.

250. Ordnance sergeants cannot be reduced to the ranks by sentence of a court-martial; but they can be discharged from service. They cannot, however, be tried by a garrison court-martial, except by special permission of the department commander. (Reg. 895.)

251. HOSPITAL STEWARD.—There are two kinds of hospital stewards allowed by law. First, those for posts and general hospitals: of these there may be enlisted as many as the Surgeon-General may require.

252. Second, to each cavalry regiment two regimental hospital stewards, Fifth Artillery one, and to the new regiments of infantry one for each battalion, called battalion hospital stewards. All these have the same rations and clothing as ordnance sergeants, and thirty-three dollars per month.

253. There is another kind of hospital steward allowed by Regulations. (Reg. 1325, and note.) An

enlisted man may be detailed, called an Acting Hospital Steward, in the absence of a competent person to be appointed. In this capacity, at posts of four companies or less he will receive twenty-five dollars per month; and, when there are more than four companies, twenty-two dollars per month.

254. Hospital stewards may be appointed from the enlisted men of the army, or may be directly enlisted for the position. When an enlisted man is to be appointed, he must be recommended by the senior medical officer, and the recommendation should be endorsed by the commanding officer of the company and of the post or detachment. None but competent men should be recommended for the permanent appointment. (Reg. 1324.) Enlisted men, thus appointed, are appointed only for the balance of their enlistment, except volunteers, who must be discharged and enlisted again in the regular service.

255. When hospital stewards are enlisted as such, they enlist for three years. The applicant for an appointment writes his own application, and accompanies it with suitable recommendation to the Surgeon-General: if he is accepted, an order will be issued directing his enlistment.

256. Hospital stewards may be re-enlisted by the commanding officer, on the recommendation of the medical officer of the post or station. He is entitled to the benefits extended to all soldiers for

re-enlisting, viz.:—two dollars per month additional for the first re-enlistment, and one dollar per month for each subsequent re-enlistment, provided the re-enlistment, in each case, takes place within one month after the expiration of his enlistment.

257. Great care should be taken in the enlistment of hospital stewards, as the position is a responsible one. The first enlistment should be between the ages of eighteen and thirty-five. The same physical qualifications are required of a hospital steward as of a recruit. He must be free from disease and able-bodied, honest, temperate, and industrious, of even temper, and devoted to the wants and patient under the whims of the sick.

258. He must have a thorough knowledge of the English language, so as to speak and write it correctly; otherwise he could not take charge of the books and records of the hospital. He must have a practical knowledge of pharmacy, sufficient to take charge of the dispensary and of surgery, be able to dress wounds and apply bandages, extract teeth, and to cup and bleed; he should also be a good cook.

259. The duties of hospital steward involve the charge of the dispensary, and the administrative duties of the hospital. Where there are several hospital stewards in the same hospital, the duties are divided. One is placed in the dispensary, who takes charge of the medicines, puts up the prescriptions, attends the surgeon in his inspections and surgical

operations, performs the minor duties of surgery, applies bandages, extracts teeth, cups and bleeds, and makes the dressings.

260. Another steward may be placed in charge of the kitchen or cooking department, who attends to the drawing of the provisions, sees that they are properly cooked, and that the victuals are distributed according to the surgeon's directions. He manages the hospital fund, makes purchases, and takes charge of the hospital stores proper.

261. Another steward, who should be the chief steward, directs the ward-masters, nurses, and attendants in their duties, attends to the police, ventilations, and warmings, calls the roll, receives the reports, and reports to the surgeon any violations of the regulations of the hospital, and any neglect of duty on the part of any of the hospital corps. He also takes charge of the hospital books, and prepares the reports.

262. In a hospital where there is but one steward, all these duties devolve upon him; and the hospital steward should therefore be familiar with all of them.* He is a non-commissioned officer, and as such ranks all the enlisted men of the line. They are subject to his orders, and he should exact implicit obedience from all composing the hospital corps, except the medical cadet.

---

*In the absence of a hospital steward for the duty, an intelligent attendant has charge of the kitchen and cooking, and is called the Hospital Commissary.

263. For the details regarding the duties of hospital stewards, see *"The Hospital Steward's Manual."*

264. Hospital stewards are subject to the Articles of War, may be tried by general court-martials and by garrison courts on the approval of the department commander, and are subject to all the punishments inflicted by courts on non-commissioned officers, except that they cannot be reduced to the ranks: they may, however, be discharged. The following Regulations must be borne in mind:

"1327. Hospital stewards, whenever stationed in places whence no post return is made to the Adjutant-General's Office, or when on furlough, will, at the end of every month, report themselves by letter to the Adjutant-General and Surgeon-General, as well as to the medical director of the military department in which they may be serving; to each of whom they will also report each new assignment to duty, or change of station, ordered in their case, noting carefully the number, date, and source of the order directing the same. They will likewise report monthly, when on furlough, to the medical officer in charge of the hospital to which they are attached.

"1328. The accounts of pay, clothing, &c. of hospital stewards must be kept by the medical officers under whose immediate direction they are serving, who are, also, responsible for certified statements of such accounts, and correct descriptive lists of such stewards, to accompany them in case of transfer,—as, also, that their final statements and certificates of discharge are accurately made out when they are, at length, discharged from service."

265. WAGONER.—Each company of cavalry, volun-

teers, and regulars, and each company of artillery
in the Fifth Regiment, is allowed one wagoner, who
is mustered as such, with the pay of a corporal of
cavalry, fourteen dollars, and the clothing and rations of a soldier. Wagoners are enlisted as soldiers,
and selected afterwards, and may, therefore, at any
time be returned to the ranks.

266. The wagoner was originally intended to
take charge of the company wagon, and formerly
one was allowed to each company. In the present
war, however, transportation has been materially
reduced, and the wagon-train placed exclusively
under the direction of the regimental quartermaster, and thus the wagoner has ceased to be under
the control of the company commander. A peace-
establishment would necessitate a return to the former custom, and the wagoner be used exclusively
by the company for the conveyance of the company
property.

267. The law with regard to wagon-masters and
wagoners for the Quartermaster's Department has
been virtually null and void, owing to the conflict-
ing allowance of pay, as given in the Acts of July 5,
1838, section 10, and August 3, 1861, section 3. The
last law allows the rank, pay, and allowances of
sergeants of cavalry (seventeen dollars) to wagon-
masters, and for wagoners the rank, pay, and allowances of corporals of cavalry. The former
allows the appointment of wagon-masters at forty

dollars per month, and three rations per day, and forage for one horse.

268. These laws, however, are not regarded; and citizens are hired as teamsters, at such salaries as are justified by the locality and the prevailing prices, by the Quartermaster's Department. They are not enlisted men, but, whilst they are employed in the field, are subject to the Rules and Articles of War, and liable to be tried by a court-martial.

269. COOKS.—The law now allows the enlistment of four African under-cooks for each company of more than thirty men; if less, two are allowed. They receive ten dollars per month, three of which may be drawn in clothing, and one ration. (See Act March 3, 1863, section 10.) They are enlisted the same as other enlisted men, and their accounts are kept in the same way: they are entered on the company muster-rolls, at the foot of the list of privates. (G. O. No. 323, 1863.)

270. These cooks are to be under the direction of a head-cook, detailed from the soldiers alternately every ten days, when the company is of less than thirty men; when the company is of more than thirty men, two head-cooks are allowed. These are quite sufficient to cook the rations for a company; and, by system and method, the comfort and subsistence of a company may be greatly improved. The frequent changing of cooks under the old system worked badly for the comfort of the soldier, and they were

often treated to unwholesome food, in consequence of the inexperience of some of the men.

271. The object of changing the head-cooks every ten days, as required by section 9, Act March 3, 1863, is to teach all the men how to cook; but it will follow that the under-cooks, who are permanently on that duty, will know more about it than the head-cooks. They will simply be held responsible that the cooking is properly performed.

272. The non-commissioned officers of those companies that have no commissary sergeant take their regular tour to superintend the issue of the provisions to the men, to see that the provisions are properly cooked, that there is no waste or pilfering, and that each soldier is served without distinction or favor. In the cavalry companies, this duty is performed by the company commissary sergeant.

SPECIAL OR EXTRA DUTY.

273. SOLDIERS may be employed on duties not strictly military, when the exigencies of the service require it, for the reason that they are incident to the operations of an army, viz.:—

As *Mechanics and Laborers, Cooks and Attendants in Hospitals, Regimental Armorers, Clerks, Officers' Servants, Pioneers, Scouts, Spies, &c. &c.*

274. It has been the custom to allow additional

pay for such duties. By section 35 of the Act of March 3, 1863, such payments have been discontinued; but by the same section the authority to order such details for special service is limited to the commanding officer of forces in the field.[*]

275. MECHANICS AND LABORERS.—The employment of mechanics and laborers is generally under the direction of a quartermaster, commissary, or engineer officer, although an officer may be specially detailed to take charge of such workmen. The soldier is then relieved from duty in his company, and takes his orders from the officer in whose department he is employed.

276. Laborers include teamsters, herders, packers, assistants, strikers, &c.; and they are usually placed under some non-commissioned officer, wagon-master, packmaster, or principal workman, through whom the officer transmits his orders and instructions to the employees.

277. The same rules of discipline and obedience apply to soldiers employed on these duties as when on military duty. Simple whim or caprice is not sufficient excuse to be relieved; and applications for such an object must be respectful, and based on some plausible reason.

278. Soldiers detailed on such duty are required

---

[*]The Third Auditor has decided that, under the authority granted in the Regulations, extra-duty pay may still be allowed, until the Regulations are changed.

to attend Sunday and monthly inspections and muster, and, if not proficient in drill, should be required to attend drills until they know their duties as soldiers.

279. COOKS AND ATTENDANTS IN HOSPITALS.—Soldiers may be placed on duty in hospitals as cooks and attendants for the sick. In these capacities they are under the direction of the surgeon of the hospital, and receive their orders and instructions from him.

280. They are usually under the immediate control of the hospital steward, who directs them in the details of their duties. The regulations for the government of the hospital guide them in their duties, appertaining principally to its police and cleanliness, the administration of medicine, and the care and feeding of the patients.

281. REGIMENTAL ARMORERS.—Regiments armed with muskets, rifles, or carbines other than the Springfield rifle model of 1855-61-63, are entitled to an armorer, for the purpose of keeping the regimental arms in repair. He can be supplied with a set of tools and extra parts by a proper requisition on the Ordnance Department. (Par. 65, instructions for making ordnance returns.)

282. Under the direction of the commanding officer, it is the duty of the armorer to keep the arms of the regiment in repair, and to take care of the tools and extra parts.

283. CLERKS.—Competent soldiers are much

called for in the various departments, as clerks, in cases where the employment of a citizen clerk is not allowed. Like other extra-duty men, they are under the direction of the officer in whose department they are detailed, and their work may involve all the knowledge from that of a simple copyist to a complete knowledge of the administrative duties of the department they are in.

284. Clerks have the best opportunity of learning the administrative duties of the army, and, consequently, have better chances for promotion than in the ranks. The management and control of men, however, can only be learned by actual experience.

285. OFFICERS' SERVANTS.—Soldiers with their own consent and that of their captain, may be taken by company officers as servants. They are, however, required to be acquainted with their military duties, to be completely armed and equipped, and to attend at inspections and reviews with their companies. (Regulations 124 and 125.)

286. The custom most generally resorted to, is for the soldier to appropriate his leisure hours to such service; and he is not excused from any of his duty with the company. A soldier cannot be required to perform any service for the private benefit of an officer or mess of officers, unless he consents and is mustered as an officer's servant. (Regulation 126.)

287. PIONEERS, SCOUTS, SPIES, EXPRESS-MEN, &C.— Soldiers are frequently employed in the foregoing

capacities, in the absence of civilians. No specific instructions can be laid down for such duties. They generally receive their orders from the authorities directing the details, and are guided by the circumstances under which they are detailed.

288. PIONEERS are soldiers detailed to precede a command on the march, for the purpose of repairing the roads, bridges, &c. The pioneer party is usually composed of details of one or two men from each company in the command, with axes, picks, and spades, and sent in rear of the advance guard, but in front of the main force. An officer is usually detailed to direct the men in their work. It is not a permanent party, but only detailed for the emergency; and when the necessity is over the men are returned to their respective companies.

289. SCOUTS AND SPIES.—It is sometimes necessary to have soldiers act as scouts and spies. This is often dangerous duty, under certain circumstances, and is, therefore, generally well rewarded. They are used to procure information of the enemy, and require peculiar fitness for the duty.

290. As long as the soldier wears his uniform, he only subjects himself to the ordinary dangers of war, principally of being captured and treated as a prisoner of war. When, however, he lays aside his uniform and assumes a citizen's dress, or other disguise, and is caught within the enemy's lines, the usual penalty is death by hanging.

291. The laying aside of his uniform, whilst it in-

creases the penalty if caught, diminishes the chances of capture; and the soldier must exercise his discretion which alternative to choose; for no officer understanding the obligations of a soldier would require him to subject himself to the penalties of a spy against his will, however much he might tempt him with the promise of reward if he accomplished his mission. A soldier, however, can be required to go within the enemy's lines in uniform when the service requires it.

292. COURIERS.—For the purpose of transmitting information rapidly, mounted soldiers are sometimes detailed as couriers, express-men, or messengers. The route to be traveled may lead through an enemy's country; and it is necessary to wear the uniform, in order to save the soldier from the penalties of a spy. The duty is very similar to that of a scout.

293. The soldier should be prepared to destroy the dispatches when in danger of capture; for which reason an intelligent man should be selected, in order that the contents of his dispatches may be made known to him verbally, so that, if he is in danger of being captured and compelled to destroy his dispatches, he may still be able to communicate their purport, if he should escape the danger which compelled him to destroy them.

NON-COMMISSIONED OFFICERS.

ORGANIZATION.

294. THE non-commissioned officers of a regiment and company, allowed by law in the various arms and regiments of the army, are as follows, viz.:—

INFANTRY AND ARTILLERY.
(Old Army.)

Non-Commissioned Staff.	*Each Company.*
One Sergeant Major.	One First Sergeant.
One Quartermaster Sergeant.	Three Sergeants.
Two Principal Musicians.	Four Corporals.

295. Volunteer regiments of infantry differ from the above in having one commissary sergeant and one hospital steward, and no principal musicians, in the non-commissioned staff, and four sergeants and eight corporals in each company.

296.   INFANTRY.
(New Army.)

Non Commissioned Staff.	*Each Company.*
Three Battalion Sergeant Majors.	One First Sergeant.
Three Battalion Quartermaster Sergeants.	Four Sergeants.
Three Battalion Commissary Sergeants.	Eight Corporals.
Three Battalion Hospital Stewards.	
One Drum-Major, or Leader of the Band.	
Two Principal Musicians.	

297.   ARTILLERY.
                    (New Army.)

Non-Commissioned Staff.   *Each Company.*
One Sergeant Major.   One First Sergeant.
Two Quartermaster Sergeants.   One Quartermaster Sergeant.
One Commissary Sergeant.   Four Sergeants.
One Hospital Steward.   Eight Corporals.
Two Principal Musicians.

Volunteer artillery differs from the above in having no principal musicians.

298.   CAVALRY.

Non-Commissioned Staff.   *Each Company.*
One Sergeant Major.   One First Sergeant.
One Veterinary Sergeant.   One Quartermaster Sergeant.
One Quartermaster Sergeant.   One Commissary Sergeant.
One Commissary Sergeant.   Five Sergeants.
Two Hospital Stewards.   Eight Corporals.
One Chief Trumpeter.
One Saddler Sergeant.

Regular and volunteer cavalry have the same.

299.   ENGINEERS.

Non-Commissioned Staff.   *Each Company.*
One Sergeant Major.   Ten Sergeants.
One Q. M. and Commissary   Ten Corporals.
  Sergeant.

ORDNANCE.

300. The Ordnance Department has no regimental organization. The enlisted men are organized into companies at the various armories and arsenals, and the master workmen are now called

sergeants. The armorers, carriage-makers, and blacksmiths are now called corporals; the artificers, privates of the first class; and the laborers, privates of the second class. The number of each is only limited by the wants of the Ordnance Department.

RANK.

301. Non-commissioned officers, like commissioned officers, rank according to date of commissions or warrants in the same grade. The different grades rank as follows, viz.—

1. Cadet and Medical Cadet.
2. Sergeant Major.
3. Regimental Quartermaster, and Commissary Sergeants.
4. Ordnance Sergeants and Hospital Stewards.
5. First Sergeant.
6. Sergeants.
7. Corporals.

302. Non-commissioned officers are all appointed by the commanding officer of the regiment; those of the company, however, are appointed on the recommendation of the company commanders. All non-commissioned officers of a regiment can be reduced by sentence of a court-martial.

303. The non-commissioned officers of a company can be reduced by the commanding officer of the regiment on the recommendation of the company

commander; but, without such a recommendation, they must be tried by a court-martial, in order that they may be reduced.

304. Cadets, medical cadets, ordnance sergeants, and hospital stewards appointed by the Surgeon-General, cannot be reduced; although they may be discharged dishonorably.

305. Each non-commissioned officer receives a certificate or warrant of his rank, signed by the commanding officer of the regiment, and countersigned by the adjutant. (Reg. 80.)

306. At depots for recruits, where there is no legal organization, temporary appointments are made, called *Lance Sergeants* and *Lance Corporals*, that by Regulations have the same authority as a duly authorized appointment, and they must be obeyed and respected accordingly. They do not, however, receive any increase of pay beyond that of a private; and, when the recruits reach their destination, the appointment ceases. The successful performance of this duty, however, as non-commissioned officer would lead to a consideration of their claim to promotion in case of a vacancy. (Reg. 971.)

307. For the purpose of ascertaining the merits of candidates, and particularly to replace absent non-commissioned officers who have not vacated their appointments, the *Lance* appointments are frequently made in the companies. Such soldiers are virtually on probation, and their succession to

the permanent appointments, when vacancies occur, necessarily depends on the manner in which they perform their duties under the acting appointment. *Lance* appointments wear the chevron of their rank, the same as legal appointments.

308. Non-commissioned officers are usually, for offenses, placed in arrest; and only in grave cases are they placed in the guard-house. (Reg. 78.) Commissioned officers only have authority to arrest non-commissioned officers.

309. Non-commissioned officers are entitled to implicit obedience from the soldiers, and they should be obeyed and respected by the men; and when a non-commissioned officer fails in obtaining this regard and obedience from the men, he fails in his most essential qualification.

310. The confidence of the soldiers in the integrity of a non-commissioned officer can only be obtained by his being rigidly just and impartial to those under him, and by keeping his temper on all occasions, and discharging his duty without passion or feeling. A non-commissioned officer who cannot control himself will find difficulty in controlling those over whom he is placed.

311. Confidence and energy are the progressive traits of the non-commissioned officer who would be successful. Let him first feel he is right, and acting in obedience to orders and instructions, and then do his duty with decision and firmness; and

success will be more certain, and failure much less discreditable.

312. Non-commissioned officers should provide themselves with a pencil and notebook in which to enter the names of men forming the details. Orders and instructions given to them verbally they should at once reduce to writing, and not trust to their memory. Lists of property placed in their charge temporarily should be entered; and, in fact, all items that it may possibly be necessary to recall should be put down in such a book.

THE CORPORAL.

313. THE appointment of corporal is the first step to promotion in the army, and may lead to the highest distinction in the military service. The corporal is usually selected from the most intelligent privates, who have been longest in the service, and who are noted for their military appearance and attention to duty.

314. The sergeants are appointed from the corporals; and they should therefore look upon their position as one of probation, and should seek to perform well their part, in order that they may be advanced.

315. The pay of corporals of cavalry, artillery, and infantry is eighteen dollars per month; in the engineers and ordnance, twenty dollars. They get

one ration per day, except the corporal of ordnance, who receives a ration and a half. They get a small increase on the allowance of clothing to a private.

316. The duties of a corporal are simple, and depend for their successful performance mainly upon his capacity to control and direct soldiers in the performance of their duty. They take charge of the smaller details for fatigue and police duty in camp and garrison duty: their most important duty is that of Corporal of the Guard. They frequently succeed to the responsibilities of sergeant in his absence, and should therefore be familiar with his duties.

317. Corporals should bear in mind that they are entitled to implicit obedience from the men placed under them; and, whilst they are not usually authorized to confine soldiers on their own judgment, they should always be sustained by their superiors in the performance of their duties, and in the execution of their office.

318. When a soldier neglects his duty towards a corporal, the corporal should at once report the fact to the first sergeant, whose duty it is either to decide in the matter, or to report it to his company commander.

319. Non-commissioned officers have it in their power at times to favor certain soldiers, that is, to relieve them from the most disagreeable part of the

duty before them, and give it to others. Such distinctions soon destroy their influence over men, and give rise to trouble and difficulty.

320. They should seek to be just towards the men, treat all alike, and when a hardship falls upon an individual he should have no grounds for thinking he has been especially selected.

321. The corporal should insist upon obedience, without being arbitrary, and should maintain his position as a non-commissioned officer firmly, but without arrogance. When he first receives his appointment, his calibre meets with the severest tests. Soldiers, for a time, will be apt to try the material he is made of, which they do in many ways, and by progressive steps, and, if not checked, will increase to a complete disregard, and terminate in an entire inefficiency of the corporal.

322. He should take the first opportunity, and make it the decisive issue that will settle once and for all that he intends to maintain his position with the jealousy of the highest grade.

323. Corporals should be living examples for the soldiers in the neatness and cleanliness of their clothing, arms, and accoutrements. They should be the first to fall into ranks at roll-calls, and should have their tents or bunks, wherever their quarters, always systematically in order.

324. They should be familiar with the "School of the Soldier," and capable of instructing the recruits in the elementary principles of tactics.

325. In the field, where it is sometimes difficult to cook for the entire company, it is divided into messes and the non-commissioned officers placed in charge of the different messes *pro rata*. They attend to drawing provisions for their mess, and are held responsible for the conduct of the mess-mates in the keeping of their tents and the care of the camp and garrison equipage in their charge.

326. CORPORAL OF THE GUARD.—This is the most important duty that falls to the corporal. He should be perfectly familiar with the duties of the sentinel, and able to instruct the members of the guard in their duties.

327. Ordinarily, a guard consists of a lieutenant and sergeant of the guard, and three corporals, one to each relief. As soon as the guard has marched on, it is divided into three reliefs. The senior corporal is assigned to the first relief, the next to the second, and the third corporal to the last relief.

328. As soon as his relief has been assigned to him, the corporal makes a list of the names and numbers, beginning on the right, the odd numbers being in the front rank, and the even numbers in the rear rank. This list is handed to the sergeant of the guard. The corporal should keep a copy of it also.

329. As soon as the list of the first relief is taken, the corporal marches it off to post it, accompanied by the corporal of the old guard. No. 1 is relieved first; he is always stationed at the

guard-house, and is not required to march round
the chain of sentinels with the relief. The other
sentinels are relieved in succession, and are required to fall in in the rear and march round in
order, at a "*Support Arms.*" The Regulations pro-
scribe:

"394. When a sentinel sees the relief approaching, he
will halt and face to it, with his arms at a shoulder. At
six paces, the corporal will command,

1. Relief.   2. HALT!

when the relief will halt and carry arms. The corporal
will then add, 'No. 1,' or 'No. 2,' or 'No. 3,' according to
the number of the post,

Arms—PORT!

The two sentinels will, with arms at *port*, then approach
each other, when the old sentinel, under the correction
of the corporal, will whisper the instructions to the new
sentinel. This done, the two sentinels will shoulder arms,
and the old sentinel will pass, in quick time, to his place
in rear of the relief. The corporal will then command,

1. Support—ARMS!   2. Forward.   3. MARCH!

and the relief proceeds in the same manner until the
whole are relieved."

330. The first relief should be posted as
promptly as possible, as both guards are kept waiting until all the sentinels have been relieved and
have joined their guards to march off. The new
guard does not "Stack Arms" until the old one has
marched off.

331. If the guard is small, there may be but one

corporal; and he then would be required to post all the reliefs, and, in all probability, there would be no officer of the guard, and the sergeant then would be the commander of the guard. When there is a corporal to each relief, each corporal parades his own relief, posts it, and instructs the sentinels in their duty. He answers the call of the sentinels of his relief for "Corporal of the Guard."

332. The reliefs are usually posted for two hours: they have, therefore, four hours off post. It may be necessary to have two or all the corporals visiting the sentinels at once. The corporals of the other reliefs may therefore be called on when the corporal whose relief is on post is absent on duty. Each corporal, however, answers the calls of his own relief as far as possible.

333. The corporal should visit his relief thoroughly the first tour by daylight, and see that the sentinels know their day-orders well, and again the first tour at night, to see that they know and perform their night-duties properly. And they should be visited at other times also, until they know and perform their duties well; for the corporal will be held responsible by the officer of the guard that the sentinels are properly instructed.

334. Corporals should remember that the only persons authorized to give them orders when on guard are the commanding officer, officer of the day, and the commissioned and non-commissioned

officers of the guard; and they take orders from no other persons.

335. The privates of the guard should make their applications to be absent from the guard, through the corporals, who are required to see that they return punctually and are not absent longer than is necessary. The corporal is held responsible that he reports to the officer of the guard all neglect of duty or disobedience of orders or instructions by members of the guard.

336. The corporal whose relief is on post at twilight receives the countersign and communicates it to the sentinels of his relief. Afterwards the countersign is communicated by the old sentinel to the new one when the relief marches round.

337. Corporals should be careful how they exercise their own discretion in reporting offences or neglect of duty by the men. It often happens that it may be wise and judicious to let the first offence pass, with the admonition that if repeated it will certainly be taken notice of. In no case should a repetition of the same offence be allowed to pass unreported, as it is sure to be followed by others.

338. In cities and towns, and in the neighborhood of camps, patrol guards are often sent out under a non-commissioned officer, to pick up soldiers absent without authority, and to correct any abuses of which soldiers may be guilty. Such patrol guards have no authority over commissioned officers, and it is not proper that such patrols should

be instructed to demand passes of officers. Such patrols may, however, give information of improper conduct on the part of officers to the officer of the guard.

339. THE CORPORAL OF POLICE.—He may be on general police or company police. On the former, he will probably be under the direction of the officer of police or sergeant, and have a detail placed under his direction to police a certain extent of ground about the camp or quarters. On company police, he will have charge of cleaning up the company parade-ground and quarters, under the instruction of the first sergeant.

340. The police party is usually turned out twice during the day,—in the morning soon after reveille, and in the afternoon before evening parade. The duty is light if regularly performed and the corporals are attentive and require the men to do their work thoroughly each time they are turned out.

341. In barracks, the duty corresponding to police in camp, is *room-orderly*. He usually goes on for a week at a time, and alternates with the duty-sergeants and corporals, occupying the same room in barracks, in regulating the police of the room. He sees that the men keep their bunks or bedsteads in order, roll up their beds, and fold their blankets neatly after reveille; that the room is swept out and prepared for the morning inspection. In winter-time, or cold weather, the police party is required to cut wood for the kitchen and

for the quarters, where the fires are used in common. The corporal superintends the party, and sees that the duty is properly performed.

342. FATIGUE.—Corporals usually have charge of the smaller details for fatigue duty. Fatigue duty includes all the irregular work that the soldier is called upon to perform from time to time. In the field, it includes working upon roads, building fieldworks, rifle-pits, &c., making or removing obstructions, duty on forage-parties, and, in fact, all the duties where details of men are required, without arms, for short periods.

343. In barracks or quarters there are many duties that call for details for fatigue, such as loading or unloading of stores, the removal of stores from one place to another, digging of graves for deceased soldiers or officers, labor on the grounds, works, or buildings of the post, &c. All such duties are usually claimed as fatigue, and the labor should be divided *pro rata* among the non-commissioned officers and the men.

344. Corporals may either have charge of a separate party or a subdivision, and receive their instructions as to what they are expected to do, and are held responsible by their superior officers for the performance of their duty.

345. They should make lists of the names of the men under them, so that they will know at any time what men are under their orders, and be able to settle any question that may come up concerning

the detail. The habit of taking notes cannot be too strongly recommended to corporals and other non-commissioned officers.

346. They are also held responsible for the tools and other implements used by the party, and should therefore take memoranda of their number, kind, and condition, and, if any are lost, broken, or injured, they should report by whom and how they were damaged, and "whether by fault of any one," when they are turned in again.

347. ARTILLERY AND CAVALRY.—What has been laid down thus far is for the corporal of infantry, and for artillery and cavalry when dismounted. Some few duties are to be noted for the corporal mounted.

348. The duty of posting mounted sentinels in the vicinity of the enemy is generally intrusted to an officer, although along an extended line non-commissioned officers can be used to post some of the less important posts. Sergeants and corporals are usually posted with the men at important points of the line, where a number of men are necessary.

349. They see that the men do not neglect their duty, and have the officers' instructions obeyed, as regards the conduct of the post, the manner in which they are to keep the look-out, and what they are to do in the event of certain things being done by the enemy.

350. They are sometimes required to visit the

sentinels of the outer chain, to see that they are on the alert, or to carry orders to them, or to relieve or reinforce them, all of which requires a clear comprehension of the orders transmitted, and a capacity for making the men understand them correctly.

351. Sentinels are liable to lose sight of the main object for which they are posted, and to turn their attention to some minor points of their instructions. Corporals should seek to impress upon them the main objects for which they are posted, and to explain to the sentinel what is important and what is secondary. Orders should not be given loosely, but with the greatest care; and the observance of the strict letter of the orders is not so important as the spirit of them.

352. Thus, a party may be posted on a road with orders to let no one go by without written authority, the object of the post being to allow no one to go by with information for the enemy. A messenger or courier may arrive with important intelligence, desiring to go within the lines, and the officer who sent him, not anticipating such orders, may not have supplied him with the required pass. It would, therefore, not be proper to stand upon the strict letter of the order, but he should be passed in, accompanied by a sentinel, to the nearest officer.

353. Some judgment is required, in posting the outer sentinels, in choosing proper positions. It should be remembered that whilst in the daytime

elevated positions afford the best view, the reverse is the case at night; and the night posts should be removed to the hollows, where, in addition to giving a view against the sky of any one approaching, the sentinel himself cannot be seen; and it is important that pickets should not expose their posts to view any more than is necessary, and, to prevent surprises, they should be changed as frequently as possible.

354. Corporals of cavalry are sometimes placed in charge of small parties to reconnoitre, commonly called patrols. Such duty requires caution, a knowledge of the country, and, most of all, good common sense. Some shrewdness may at times be exercised in getting information from the inhabitants, in the enemy's country.

355. The object of the patrol may be specific or general: in either case, every thing should be observed in order that all possible questions about the route taken may be anticipated,—the roads, houses, streams, their distance apart, the character of the country, the disposition of the inhabitants, &c., and, in fact, every feature that could affect troops advancing or retreating.

356. In making a report on returning, a distinction should be made between what is actually seen, and what is only conjecture or report, giving in each instance the authority. All exaggeration should be avoided; but no objection can be had to laying stress upon whatever is considered particularly important.

357. The corporal should keep his patrol together as much as possible, and not permit his men to straggle or pursue any object of curiosity or interest of their own, and should especially guard against depredations or pillage. Private property even of enemies is respected by the laws of war, and its capture and appropriation are never justifiable unless ordered by higher authority and for public use. It may be necessary here and there to detach a man; but, as a rule, the patrol should keep together as much as possible for the sake of mutual support.

358. When the object of the patrol is specific, every other consideration should yield to that object. That is, the opportunity to do something else perhaps creditable should not be undertaken if the success of the patrol for the particular object would be endangered thereby.

359. Thus, an opportunity to capture a patrol of the enemy might present itself. On the advance it would rarely be justifiable, but on the return it might be undertaken, if in case of failure the information obtained would still be transmitted and the object of the patrol completed.

360. Strict caution is sometimes necessary. By-roads and unfrequented paths should be traveled, or, if necessary, roads should be entirely avoided. If the object of the patrol is important, no superior force or obstacles should be regarded as a good ex-

cuse for abandoning the object and returning, and there must be no *supposed* impossibility. The attempt must be made, and failure ascertained beyond a doubt. If driven back or pursued by the enemy, as soon as he gives up the pursuit the object of the patrol must be resumed.

361. Stable-guards are peculiar to artillery and cavalry. Corporals and duty-sergeants alternate on this detail. Usually a non-commissioned officer and three men are sufficient. They do not march on, like the other guard, are not armed, and do not challenge.

362. Their duty is to watch the horses that none get loose and escape, and that they do not injure themselves. The non-commissioned officers are responsible that the guard is properly posted and regularly relieved. They go on at retreat, and are relieved at reveille.

363. Horses escaping through the neglect of the stable-guard should be charged to them and deducted from their pay. They may be charged to the entire guard, each paying his share; or, where it can be ascertained what particular sentinel permitted the horse to escape, the amount may be charged exclusively to him.

364. Corporals of artillery usually act as gunners, and assist the chief of piece in managing the gun and directing the cannoneers. The piece may be aimed either by the gunner or the chief of piece.

THE SERGEANT.

365. IT is difficult to draw the line between the duties of the corporal and those of the sergeant. There is really no great difference in their duties. Sergeants generally have larger details under their charge, and have corporals under their direction to assist them. They are usually intrusted with more responsible duties, and they are supposed to have greater experience, and to approach nearer the commissioned officer in a knowledge of all military matters.

366. Sergeants generally have a more general supervision of the men, whilst corporals have more of the detail to attend to. The company should be divided into a number of squads proportionate to the number of duty-sergeants in the company, with a proportionate number of corporals, who should have charge when the sergeants are absent.

367. They are responsible for the camp and garrison equipage which the squad has in general use. They have charge of the preliminary instruction of the men in their various duties, and must preserve order in their squad, and see that the men do not absent themselves without proper authority.

368. The most important duty of sergeant is that of file-closer. Posted in the rear of the company when paraded, it is his duty to see that the

men pay attention to their duty, preserve order, march properly, and keep closed.

369. In time of battle, it is his duty to keep the men in ranks, not to allow them to fall out on any pretext, and to prevent them from misbehaving before the enemy. He is even required to shoot men down when they attempt to run away in times of danger.

370. The men must not be permitted to fall out to attend the wounded without orders; the battle must be won first, and then the wounded can be taken care of without endangering the safety of the entire command.

371. On the march he must see that the men do not fall out unnecessarily, and, when absolutely necessary, that the soldier turns over his gun and accoutrements to a comrade to be carried until he can overtake his company again.

372. He must see that the men fill their canteens with water, and not whiskey, before the march commences, and that they do not eat up their rations at improper hours on the march; for the habit of munching at all hours on the march, besides being injurious to the health of the soldier, may defeat the purpose of an expedition based on the necessity that a limited supply of food must last a given number of days.

373. Sergeants are usually appointed, by the commanding officer of the regiment or post, from

the corporals, on the recommendation of the company commander.

374. In advancing non-commissioned officers from one grade to another, no claim of seniority is considered, except where the merits of the two candidates are equal; then the senior in date should be appointed. The pay of duty-sergeants of infantry, cavalry, and artillery is seventeen dollars per month, with an allowance of clothing and one ration.

375. SERGEANT OF THE GUARD.—The sergeant of the guard has general supervision of the corporals and members of the guard. He sees that the reliefs are turned out at the proper time, that the corporals obey the calls of the sentinels, receives the prisoners and sees that they are properly secured, that sentences of prisoners are carried out each day, prepares the guard report for the officer of the guard, and, in general, is responsible that all the members of the guard under him perform their duty.

376. Where the posts are numerous, sergeants assist the corporals in posting the sentinels. They must see that the corporals comprehend the orders and are capable of instructing the sentinels; and when a sentinel calls for the corporal of the guard, it is the duty of the sergeant to see that the corporal obeys the call promptly.

377. The sergeant carries the keys of the prisons, sees that the prisoners are duly locked up at night

and sent out to work in the morning, and that those sentenced to close confinement on bread and water are not visited or fed by any of the other prisoners or members of the guard. When prisoners are brought to the guard-house to be confined, he takes charge of them, takes down their names, company, and regiment, the charges against each, by whom preferred, and by whose order confined.

378. Prisoners undergoing sentence he must attend to, and see that the penalty is executed; also that those whose sentences expire are reported to the officer of the guard or officer of the day, in order that they may be released; also that the prisoners are supplied by the cooks with their victuals. Prisoners are usually supplied from their company by the cooks. Citizen prisoners, or prisoners of war, are either assigned to some of the companies, where their rations are cooked, or else, where they are numerous, some one is detailed to cook for them.

379. The sergeant should verify the list of prisoners, and see that they are all present when he marches on guard. He should also see that all the articles on the guard-book, for which he or the officer of the guard receipts, are on hand. These are, usually, the furniture of the guard-room, the utensils for labor used by the prisoners, and the handcuffs or shackles, &c.

380. The guard report is usually made out in a Guard Report Book, furnished from post or regimental head-quarters. In the absence of such a

book, a report must be ruled out on a sheet of foolscap, according to the prescribed form in the Regulations, page 63.

381. Whatever happens during the tour of guard is mentioned in the column of remarks. These are usually the visits of the officer of the day, the visits of the officer of the guard to the sentinels, the manner in which they have performed their duty, and the incidents of note that have occurred during the tour.

382. The attention of the commanding officer may also be called to any changes that may be thought necessary of matters or things over which the officer of the day or officer of the guard exercises supervision. When there is no officer of the guard, the report is signed by the sergeant and countersigned by the officer of the day.

383. In the absence of cavalry, infantry is sometimes used on picket-duty, to furnish the outer sentinels, particularly where the contending armies are in close proximity, as immediately preceding a battle, or during a siege.

384. In this case, the same precautions are necessary in selecting positions, remaining concealed, and being constantly on the alert, as are enjoined upon cavalry. The same system of posting and relieving sentinels is pursued. The sentinels patrol in the same way in the night and during foggy weather.

385. During the day it is not generally considered

proper to patrol. The sentinels are usually posted in commanding positions, where they have a good view to the front, and can see the posts on the right and left.

386. Sometimes, especially where the men would be exposed to the enemy's fire, the reliefs are dispensed with, and the three sentinels of each post are posted together and relieve each other,— two sleeping on their arms, whilst the third keeps watch. This is particularly recommended in Indian warfare.

387. When cavalry is used for the outer sentinels, the infantry is usually posted in small detachments in rear, each under an officer or non-commissioned officer, according to its strength, forming a line of supports to which the vedettes retire on the approach of a superior force, and with which they are connected by a chain of sentinels within call of each other.

388. POLICE.—The policing of camp is usually performed by two kinds of details. The roster for the company police is kept in the company, and the duty-sergeants and the corporals alternate in taking charge of this detail, whose duty it is to police the company-grounds twice a day, and they are turned out by the non-commissioned officer when the police-call sounds.

389. General police is usually performed by the guard which has marched off the morning previous; and the duty of this detail is to police the grounds

in general use by all the regiment or detachment, the quarters of the field officers, and, generally, to perform all the clearing up that it is necessary to do outside of the company-grounds. The police-call sounds usually twice during the day,—once in the morning, immediately after reveille, and again in the afternoon, just before retreat parade.

390. The sergeant of the guard that has marched off the previous morning parades his men, and, with the corporals to assist him, proceeds to collect all the rubbish that has accumulated since the last detail, and to do any other cleaning that the officer of police may direct. Sometimes the officer of the day acts as officer of police, and gives the instructions to the sergeant.

391. This duty is performed by collecting the rubbish in heaps by one part of the detail, whilst another portion is engaged with handbarrows in transporting it to some place of general deposit, where, if necessary, it may be again removed in wagons.

392. The men who are absent from this detail from sickness, or any other legitimate cause, are not usually replaced. It is, however, the duty of the non-commissioned officers to see that all the members of the old guard parade, or are properly excused.

393. Where prisoners are numerous, the general police may be dispensed with, and the work be performed by the prisoners, under the direction of the

provost-sergeant; and this is usually the case where there is no other work for the prisoners to be employed at.

394. A provost-sergeant is one who is detailed permanently to take charge of the prisoners, to attend to the execution of sentences, and perform all the duties relating to the prisoners prescribed for the non-commissioned officers of the guard. He is often charged with making arrests of non-commissioned officers and soldiers.

395. In barracks, besides being chiefs of squads, sergeants take their turns with the corporals, a week at a time, as room-orderlies, and are required to keep the room in order, and see that the men have every thing prepared for inspection every morning. (See Par. 341.)

396. The kitchen must be supplied with wood and water. This may be done either by special details for the purpose each day, or by the company police. In either case a sergeant or corporal is in charge of the party, and is responsible that the wood and water are properly furnished.

397. FATIGUE.—Sergeants are usually placed in charge of larger details for fatigue than corporals and have perhaps one or more corporals to assist them. The same general principles that are laid down for corporals on fatigue duty apply to sergeants. The sergeant may be under the direction of an officer immediately over him, or may have

exclusive charge of the party and of the execution of the duty.

398. Fatigue duty, including as it does the entire range of labor likely to fall to the lot of troops, may sometimes require peculiar knowledge and special experience. The construction of a bridge, the repairing of a railroad, or the management of a boat, at a critical moment when there is no time to look for competent men, may involve a success the accomplishment of which might win an undying laurel for some sergeant who has stored up the knowledge or experience for the favorable moment.

399. On all occasions of police, fatigue, or guard duty, the details are marched to and from their work in an orderly and military manner; and any disorderly conduct or neglect of duty on the part of the men should be promptly reported for punishment. The neglect to enforce these minor requirements of service soon leads to more serious dereliction of duty.

400. ARTILLERY AND CAVALRY.—The sergeants, like the corporals, of cavalry and artillery, have duties not common to infantry, that require to be separately enumerated. The sergeant of artillery is generally chief of piece. He has charge of the gun, sees that it is kept clean and in order, that the implements are in constant repair and always in their proper places, and that the carriages are covered with tarpaulins when not in use. He directs the

movements of the piece at drills and on the march, and superintends its service at practice-firing and in action.

401. In battle, the importance of the position of chief of piece can scarcely be overestimated. No individual soldier in the army is required to be so cool or under stronger obligations to preserve unimpaired all his faculties. The proximity of danger, the deafening uproar, the confusion of frightened horses, and the sometimes fearful effectiveness of the enemy's artillery upon his battery, test his capacity for the position to the utmost; and to remain collected, and go through the sighting and direct the loading and firing of the gun without excitement or mistake, at such a time, is undoubtedly the most sublime achievement of the individual soldier. To estimate the distance, sight the gun, direct the length of fuse and kind of shot, with such rapidity as is sometimes necessary, and all the while be able to check the excitement, and prevent the errors of the cannoneers, is a task that has no parallel in the service.

402. Duty-sergeants of artillery and cavalry take their tour with the corporals on stable-guard. There are two important duties of the cavalry soldier in which sergeants and corporals perform an important part: these are outpost and mounted patrol duty.

403. In outpost duty the non-commissioned officers are used in posting and relieving the vedettes;

and sometimes they have charge of small, isolated stations, and are held responsible that the duty is properly performed by them and the men under them. Much depends on the care and attention with which they instruct the sentinels in their duty, and their capacity for making them comprehend the orders.

404. They should be particularly careful in cautioning the sentinels not to give unnecessary alarm, and never to fire until they feel assured of what they are firing at, and that there is some probability of their shots being effective. Many an innocent person has been killed by the sentinel, in his trepidation, neglecting or forgetting to challenge, and firing without first ascertaining whether it was friend or foe who was approaching.

405. Many false alarms have been produced, and serious consequences have resulted, from firing unnecessarily, sometimes at friends accidentally in the way, or at officers visiting the posts, sometimes at hogs, cattle, or other animals, and frequently at nothing at all. Many of these accidents can be prevented by the judgment, coolness, and alertness of the non-commissioned officers.

406. Sometimes small posts are established on the roads or lines of approach, and the party is placed under the direction of a sergeant or corporal. This kind of duty is highly important, and requires the utmost discretion of the non-commissioned officer to guard against surprise, and send timely notice

to the rear of the movements of the enemy, and at the same time to prevent unnecessary alarm, so that a small force making a dash at the post may not have all the effect of a reconnaissance in force.

407. Therefore the approach of a small force should be resisted as long as there is a possibility of keeping it back; and a bold front will often keep back a very superior force; for if the post has been properly selected, and the necessary precautions have been taken to conceal the strength of the party, the enemy is very apt to suppose that they are well supported. Information sent to the rear should be facts, and not conjecture; and, if the report cannot be sent in writing, a reliable and clear-minded messenger should be intrusted with the duty.

408. A thorough knowledge of the locality, and the routes by which the post may be approached, as well as of the disposition and feelings of the inhabitants, their number, and where they live, should be obtained. The people in the vicinity should be warned to remain about their homes, and positively not to visit the post or attempt to pass beyond the lines in the direction of the enemy; they should also be prohibited from visiting the adjoining houses, and, when necessary, cautioned about revealing to the enemy any information about the locality of the post or the numbers or intentions of the party. Frequent changes of position are recommended; the best time for making these changes is just after dark, and at daybreak.

409. The watering and feeding of the horses should be performed by not more than one-third of the party at once; and, if it is necessary to go any distance to water, the men should take every thing with them. The men should always be prepared to be in the saddle in the shortest possible time. They should not sleep at night at all; during the day a portion of the men should sleep whilst the others watch. The fact must always be borne in mind that a surprise has no apology.

410. Mounted patrol duty requires the greatest combination of daring, intrepidity, caution, judgment, and intelligence, that a sergeant or corporal can possess. Only general directions can be given for this duty, as it would be impossible to anticipate every case or provide for every emergency.

411. The object of the patrol may be to ascertain a particular piece of information, or simply to proceed, if practicable, to a particular point, or as far as possible, to ascertain the vicinity of the enemy, or the character of the country, or the amount of forage, or to acquire any other general information that might be of service.

412. If the patrol is small and composed of only six or eight men, they march without advance or rear guard. Passing through thick woods, it might be well to send two men fifty or a hundred yards in advance. The patrol should avoid the highways and frequently-travelled routes, and should seek to keep themselves concealed as much as possible.

413. They must avoid building fires; and to feed their horses and rest themselves they should seek out thickets and deep ravines off the road, and station a look-out concealed from view. If an inhabitant falls in with the patrol whilst resting, he should be held until the party is ready to move on. In making inquiries of the people, care should be taken to ask the questions in such a way that they shall not be able to conjecture the object of the patrol.

414. The enemy should be avoided, and no attempt should be made to take prisoners when it would endanger the expedition. If pursued by the enemy, they should seek to make their escape; and if driven off their route, it should be resumed when the enemy give up the pursuit. The object of the expedition should not be abandoned for any trivial reason, or as long as there is a hope of accomplishing it.

415. A patrol sent to ascertain whether an enemy occupy a certain position, and desiring to know in what strength, may do so by a little boldness and rapidity of action. They approach as close as they can at a walk, and with as little noise as possible, for which purpose the sabres should be strapped to the saddle on the left side, the hilt coming up near the pommel, to prevent rattling.

416. As soon as they appear in sight of the vedettes, they make a dash at them, to capture them if possible, and certainly to drive them in upon their

support; and, if the force is not too large for them, they attack it also. Here they should halt, particularly if the support retires in good order and with obstinacy. They should remain until they hear the alarm in the camp of the enemy.

417. The number of drums, bugles, and trumpets will furnish a very good indication of the strength of the enemy. The enemy will be at a loss to know whether it is an attack in force or a feint; and the interval before they find out should be used to get beyond pursuit. Larger patrols would generally be under the direction of a commissioned officer, who of course should know the customary manner of marching and conducting patrols, unless he has entirely omitted to learn his simplest duties.

418. The Color-Sergeant.—In each regiment a sergeant is selected for his gallantry and military bearing, to carry the regimental colors. He is accompanied by a color-guard, composed of five corporals, who are also distinguished for their military conduct. They parade with the colors on all occasions when the regiment is formed for the march, parade, review, or for battle. The sergeant is in the front rank, the two senior corporals are on the right and left of the sergeant, and the three junior corporals are in the rear rank. The post of the color-guard is on the left of the right center company. All the romance and heroism of the regiment centre in the color-guard and the emblem with which they are intrusted. On it are inscribed the

battles in which the regiment has participated and which recall the deeds it has performed. Much depends upon the courage and daring of the color-sergeant. Wherever he will carry the flag, the men will follow to protect and defend it; and no non-commissioned officer occupies a post that is so likely to bring distinction and promotion if he does his duty; whilst none is more certain to bring disgrace if he proves recreant to his trust.

THE FIRST SERGEANT.

419. The duties of first sergeant are peculiar to his position, and require capacity and knowledge superior to those of other sergeants. Whilst he does not rank as high as some others, nor receive as much pay, his position is one of the most responsible and most honorable that non-commissioned officers can occupy.

420. The first sergeant is selected by the captain of the company from the other sergeants, without regard to rank, and commissioned by the commanding officer of the regiment. He may be reduced, like other non-commissioned officers, by the commanding officer on the recommendation of the company commander, or by sentence of a court-martial. The pay of first sergeants of artillery, cavalry, and infantry is twenty-four dollars per month, with one ration and an allowance of clothing.

421. He has the immediate supervision of the

company. He gets his orders from the captain or officer commanding the company, and sees that they are performed in the company. He is, in fact, the foreman; the men are the artisans. He lays out and superintends the details of the work which the captain has directed to be executed.

422. Orders received from the commanding officer or other officer by the first sergeant should be communicated to the company commander at once, before being obeyed, if there is time. Under any circumstances, they should be reported to him as soon as possible. Whenever the orderly call sounds, the first sergeant repairs to regimental or post head-quarters to receive the orders or instructions, and, if they are at all unusual, they should be communicated to the company commander without delay.

423. An hour is generally established for assembling the orderlies or first sergeants, usually at noon, for the distribution of orders and announcement of details, and for communicating any alteration in the ordinary routine. The published orders should be copied in the company order-book; and it is best, also, to make memorandums of any other orders or instructions received.

424. He keeps the rosters, and makes all the details: he superintends the company clerk, and assists him in making out all the required papers. These duties are fully explained in "The Company Clerk," and are, therefore, omitted here.

425. He should memorize the roster of the company in alphabetical order, so that he can at all hours form the company and call the roll, day or night. Much natural shrewdness is required in this duty, to associate in the memory the name, face, and voice of the soldier and his proper position in the ranks; for the men are frequently in the habit of answering for absentees, and if they find that the sergeant can be deceived in this respect they are very likely to practise it on him.

426. There should be a uniform method of forming the company; and there is no reason why there should be a difference in the different corps or in different regiments. The company should be sized. In all the odd-numbered companies the tallest men are placed on the right, diminishing in size to the left, and in the even-numbered companies the tallest should be on the left, diminishing to the right,—the principle being that in each division the tallest men should be on the flanks, and the shortest in the center: the regimental front will thus present a level line, and there will be an apparent uniformity in size of the entire regiment.

427. At all roll-calls the first sergeant takes his place six or eight paces, according as the company is small or large, in front of and opposite the centre of his company, facing towards it. If the company is forming without arms, the men fall in and take the position of *parade rest*, and the first sergeant takes the same position. (Reg. 335.)

428. They should fall in in two ranks, whether with or without arms. With arms they fall in at a shoulder arms instead of at parade rest. The company is formed in the interval between the *musician's call* and the last note of the *assembly* when every man should be in ranks; and those who fall in afterwards should be punished for being late.

429. When the music has ceased, the first sergeant commands "*Attention!*" whereupon the company, if at parade rest, take *the position of the soldier*, and if with arms, the sergeant adds, "*Support arms.*" The roll is then called, commencing with sergeants, Adams, Smith, &c., in the order of rank, until all are called; then "*corporals,*" Brown, Jones, &c., to "*farriers;*" then "*buglers, or musicians;*" and finally "*privates,*" Ames, Brown, Cox, &c., in alphabetical order. As each name is called, they answer, "*Here;*" and if with arms at a support they come to a "shoulder" and finally to "order arms," immediately on answering to their names; if with sabres or pistols drawn, they return them to their scabbards.

430. After the roll has been called, the first sergeant turns to the officer superintending the roll-call, and reports the absentees by name. If none are absent without proper authority, he reports, "*All present or accounted for.*" If the officer should then take command of the company, the first sergeant takes his post on the right of the company and acts as right guide.

431. The first sergeant makes out the morning report and signs it, and then submits it to the commanding officer of the company for his signature, after which it is handed in to the regimental or post commander. To make it correctly the sergeant should be constantly posted on the changes in the company, as the report is valuable only in proportion to its correctness. It should be a correct statement of the company, in order that the commanding officer may each day be able to know the condition of his command.

432. The sick report must always be made up in the morning before the morning report, in order that the report may be accurate as to the number of men *for duty. For duty* means all the men available for the legitimate duties of the soldier; and the column "for duty" should show the effective strength for actual service of the company for each day. Some understanding is necessary with regard to the men on extra and daily duty, as to whether they are included in the effective strength or not. An order from post or regimental head-quarters would regulate this point.

433. The first sergeant should be quartered with the men, and, when possible, has a separate room or tent. He has general supervision of all the company property,—the quartermaster and commissary sergeant assisting him in the details. He keeps rosters of all the property issued to the men and non-

commissioned officers, and sees that the surplus property is cared for and properly stored.

434. He must see that the quartermaster and commissary sergeants do their duty with regard to the property and that they hand in to him statements of all the property received and issued, lost or destroyed, in order that the records of the company may be correctly kept.

435. He sees that all the other non-commissioned officers do their duty; he holds the chiefs of squads responsible for the condition of their respective squads, and reports to the captain when any one neglects his duty in any respect.

436. He is usually empowered by the captain to confine soldiers and arrest non-commissioned officers for offences. In these cases he always reports the confinement or arrest to be by order of the captain or company commander. He should, however, report the facts in the case to the captain or company commander at once, in order that he may be prepared to sustain him in the act, or correct it if he does not approve of his action.

437. He makes all the details from the company, and sees that a record is kept on the roster. He parades the details, inspects them, and sees that they are properly equipped for the duty they are to perform, and then turns them over to a non-commissioned officer to be marched to their posts, or marches them there himself. He generally marches on the guard detail himself. (Reg. 376.)

438. After parading and inspecting it, and having ascertained that the guard are all in proper condition, he marches them to the usual place for mounting the guard, where the sergeant-major receives them. The detail is formed in two ranks, the supernumeraries being in a third rank. When he arrives on the ground, he forms his detail on the left of other details that may have already arrived, faces it to the front, and brings it to "*rear open order*," and, after commanding "*front*," reports his detail, "*all present*" or "*corporal* or *private* so-and-so *absent*," as the case may be, and then takes post in rear of his own supernumeraries, in rear of the guard, where he remains at parade rest until the guard marches off, when he marches his supernumeraries back to the company-ground. (Reg. 383.)

439. Supernumeraries, usually one or two, are detailed to take the place of members of the guard from the company who fall sick during the tour. The supernumerary receives credit for a tour if he takes the place of any one on the guard, no matter at what time of the tour. The supernumeraries are, therefore, the next for guard after the detail is made. (For the manner of keeping the rosters and making the details, see "Company Clerk," Par. 20.)

440. The most responsible duties of first sergeant are those which involve the issue and care of public property and keeping an account thereof. These are principally the issuing of arms and ammunition,

and camp and garrison equipage to the men; the keeping of a record to whom and when issued, and the charging of articles lost, or procuring affidavits or certificates if the articles are not lost through the fault of any one; the issuing and keeping an account of clothing; the drawing and issuing of the rations, including the care and disposition of the company savings, and disbursement of the company fund if—as sometimes happens—it be intrusted to him; and, finally, the care of the company property, usually accumulated for the use of the company by purchases with the company fund.

441. These duties are materially facilitated by numbering the men in the company as nearly as possible in alphabetical order; and a man should not be permitted to change his number as long as he remains with the company. (Reg. 90.)

442. The company should be provided with a complete set of marking-implements, so that each article may be marked with the letter of the company, and the number of the man who uses it, and, in some cases, his name or initials. These implements are purchased with the company fund, and usually consist of a set of stencil-plates, a brand of the letter of the company and punch of the same, and a set of numbers for both, to mark articles of wood or iron. The completeness and perfection of these articles add greatly to the security of the company property and to the protection of individuals in the company.

443. *Ordnance.*—The design is that a company shall draw its full allowance of ordnance; and it is expected to appertain to the company as long as it is serviceable. The regimental armorer keeps it in repair; and such repairs as cannot be made by him may be made by sending to the nearest arsenal. The Ordnance Department requires that the old arms shall be inspected, condemned, and ordered to be turned in before new arms can be drawn.

444. A strict account of the arms, therefore, is necessary, and tends to keep them in good order; for if the soldiers find that they are to pay for every loss or deficiency, they will take as much care of them as if they were their own personal property. The arms should bear the letter of the company and be numbered, and each soldier should have his corresponding number issued to him. If the arms cannot be so lettered and numbered from the arsenal, it can be done by the regimental armorer.

445. The surplus arms not issued to the soldiers are kept in repair, and are boxed up and placed in store usually at the post to which the company belongs. The storing is done by the quartermaster sergeant, if there is one to the company. If there is not a company store-room to which he alone has access, the boxes are turned over to the quartermaster for storage, who gives a storage receipt therefore. The boxes should be marked with the letter of the company, the name of the officer

accountable for the property, and a list of the contents.

446. When ordnance is sent to the arsenal for repairs, it is boxed up in the same way, and marked for the arsenal to which it is to go. Triplicate invoices are made out, one of which is sent direct to the officer in charge of the arsenal, and the other two to the quartermaster to whom the ordnance is turned over for transportation, who gives transportation receipts for the same. The invoices should be minute as to the nature of repairs required on each article.

447. A record of the articles issued to each soldier is kept; and where an article differently numbered is issued to him, it should be noted, or else the number should be changed, if there is no other article of the same kind similarly numbered in the company. The foregoing applies to all articles of ordnance, including horse-equipments, &c. (See "Company Clerk," Par. 41.)

448. *Clothing.*—Clothing is accounted for differently from any other property. It is issued to the soldiers, and their receipt is taken on receipt-rolls, which become the vouchers for the officer accountable for the property.

449. The quartermaster is required to keep the clothing on hand, from whom it is drawn on requisitions signed by the company commander. The amount of clothing required for each issue is ascer-

tained by actual inspection; and the actual wants of the soldier should determine his allowance.

450. An officer should be present at the issue to witness the signature of each soldier. If there is no officer, a non-commissioned officer must do it. The articles drawn are entered on the receipt-roll, opposite the soldier's name, under their respective headings, and he signs his name opposite, and opposite to it is the signature of the witness, repeated to each signature of the men.

451. These receipt-rolls are made in duplicate, one of which is retained by the officer accountable for the clothing, and the other is forwarded, as a voucher to his returns, to the Quartermaster-General.

452. The money value of each issue is computed and entered in the clothing-book on the page appropriated to the soldier, with the date of issue, and his receipt or signature witnessed as on the receipt-roll. The price is obtained from the General Order, published periodically, giving the price of the clothing for the army.

453. Frequent inspections should be had of the men's clothing, in order that the soldiersmay be prevented from disposing of their clothing improperly; and as it is both contrary to law and Regulations for soldiers to sell their clothing, such offences should be rigidly punished. (Act March 3, 1863, sec. 23, and Art. 38.)

454. *Camp and Garrison Equipage.*—This kind of property, although borne on the return with

clothing, is differently accounted for, being reported on hand as company property until worn out, when it is inspected and condemned and ordered to be dropped. Soldiers are not required to pay for its loss, except when lost or destroyed through their fault or neglect.

455. A record of the issues to the soldiers is kept the same as of ordnance. (See Form 5, "Company Clerk," Par. 41.) The property used in common by squads is issued to the chiefs of squads, whose duty it is to look after the property and report any loss or destruction of it, in order that it may be charged to the proper person if lost or destroyed through the fault or neglect of any one.

456. Cavalry and artillery companies have also a certain amount of quartermaster's property, which is accounted for on a separate return, in the same manner as camp and garrison equipage. Where there is a quartermaster sergeant in the company, he is usually intrusted with the transportation and storage of all surplus company property.

457. *Rations.*—If there is a commissary sergeant in the company, the immediate labor and duty of drawing the rations and distributing them is intrusted to him; otherwise this is superintended by the first sergeant.

458. The ration is a legal allowance, and the soldier cannot arbitrarily be deprived of it. Yet it has been frequently withheld from the soldier in part, under various pretences, particularly where

the provisions were not on hand for issue at the time.

459. This is manifestly unjust; and no circumstances can justify the retaining of such rations, even where the full rations cannot be issued; for in such cases the deficiency should be commuted in money.

460. Every regimental or post commissary can provide for the full issue, or, in lieu thereof, can pay the money-commutation; and commanding officers should be appealed to where they neglect or omit to do so.

461. When there are no funds on hand with which to commute back rations or such portions as are not on hand for issue, the commissary should give certificates to the companies of the amounts due, which may be issued subsequently, or commuted. This commutation-money on the savings of the rations forms the principal source from which the company fund is derived; and by a judicious management of this fund the comfort of the men may be materially enhanced.

462. A prudent administration of it depends very much on the first sergeant, as the company commander is greatly dependent on him for its proper disbursement. He calls the attention of the company commander to the requirements of the men, suggests what is needed, ascertains where it can be most economically obtained, makes the purchases,

and submits the bills to the company commander for payment.

463. The savings of the rations can be sold to the commissary only. (Reg. 1188 and 1234.) There are other sources of revenue to the company that go to increase the company fund. At posts on the frontier, and at permanent stations, the cultivation of a garden, whilst it increases the savings of the ration, may also produce a surplus, which may be sold and the proceeds added to the company fund. So also with the proceeds of any sale of company property.

464. The cooking of the ration is an important duty, and greatly depends on the knowledge and experience of the non-commissioned officers; for in the absence of a commissary sergeant the sergeants and corporals take turns in superintending the cooks. (See Cooks, Par. 269.)

465. *Company Property.*—By this is meant, in addition to the public property issued to the company, all those articles purchased by the company fund, or manufactured in the company. Such are the company desk and mess-chest, mechanics' tools, marking-implements, mess-furniture, company library, &c.

466. By an economical administration of this kind of property the comfort and harmony of a company of soldiers are greatly increased. They feel that the acquisition of such articles is intended

for their good, and each man performs his part in taking care of them.

467. The company desk is a necessary article of furniture for every company, in which the records of the company are kept. It is in the personal charge of the first sergeant, and should be made with compartments and drawers for the books, papers, and stationery necessary for a company and requires to be kept with method and order, to facilitate the making out of the various papers required for a company. It should be portable, and have a lid to turn down on which to write, so that it may be set up at any time or place for use.

468. A mess-chest is another necessary article of furniture; and the ingenuity of soldiers has been taxed from time immemorial to make this article, as well as the company desk, in the greatest perfection.

469. Different circumstances and conditions require different modifications; and none have yet been invented to suit every case in which it is liable to be used. Large chests are inconvenient on account of transportation, and a small one does not contain sufficient.

470. A number of small ones, according to the size of the company, small enough to be easily handled by two men, and conveniently arranged for carrying the small rations and the mess-furniture, have been found to be the best.

471. The mess-furniture may be from the simplest kind which is usually used in the field, to a complete

hotel establishment, according to the location and circumstances of the company. At permanent posts they can be well situated in this respect, and have every convenience necessary. When required to move, if not able to take the mess-furniture with them, it can be sold, and a new supply obtained at their place of destination.

472. Tools and implements of various kinds are found to be very useful in a company. In the field, against the enemy, the supply must necessarily be very limited; but in time of peace a full supply of almost every kind may be accumulated for the general benefit.

473. To enumerate some of them, they are suggested in the order of their importance:—A set of marking-implements, a set of carpenter's tools, a set of blacksmith's tools, a sewing-machine, shoemaker's tools, tinner's tools, garden-implements, seine or fish nets, &c.

474. A cow, to furnish milk in the coffee, may often be conveniently kept, and several pigs may be fattened every month or two on the slops from the kitchen. A small library of well-selected books is quite an acquisition to the company, gives occupation and entertainment to the men during their leisure hours, and has a tendency to keep them about their company quarters.

475. The foregoing will give some idea to what extent and perfection the administration of a com-

pany can be carried. The company is a small colony, which can live in peace, harmony, and comfort or be disturbed by internal commotions and discomforts unendurable, depending, perhaps, more on the first sergeant than on any other person in the company. Much depends upon the captain; but without a competent sergeant to execute his plans, any benevolent designs on his part for the improvement of the company would be difficult to carry into execution.

476. There is no material difference in the duties of the first sergeant in the three arms of infantry, artillery, and cavalry, except some few modifications incident to the different kinds of arms used and the peculiar nature of the service.

477. In artillery and cavalry, some additional responsibility in the increased amount of property, different tactics, the less compact rather more straggling nature of the duties to be performed and the consequent difficulty of less discipline of the men, are the principal features which the first sergeant has generally to overcome, or should at least be familiar with before he attains to the charge of the company.

478. The first sergeant, although he should be familiar with all the duties of the sergeants and corporals, is seldom called upon to perform any duty that would remove him from the duties of his own position. He is, therefore, not liable for guard-duty, or fatigue or detached service, unless

the entire company is on the same. He is, however, not absolutely excluded from any special service of short duration that it may be desirable, under peculiar circumstances, to intrust him with.

479. The most important task of the first sergeant relates to the government of the company and the preservation of good order and military discipline. This depending chiefly on innate qualifications, definite rules, cannot easily be given. A complete control of temper, good judgment, and a strong sense of justice are essential; whilst a due application to duty and attention to the necessities of the men are also of the highest importance.

480. Whilst he is not expected to preserve the same distance between himself and the men that exists between them and the officer, his position, indeed, not allowing of it, he should, however, never descend to familiarity, but should always endeavor to preserve a certain amount of restraint, and select his intimates from the first sergeants of other companies or non-commissioned officers of merit of other grades.

481. A quiet, imperturbable temper, combined with firmness and resolution, will of itself enforce obedience and command respect. Excitability and passion cannot easily be divested of prejudice and injustice, and have a tendency to excite similar feelings in the men.

482. Partiality and favor to individuals should be avoided above all things. The men should be

treated with the greatest equality. Harsh and violent treatment, even towards the worst of soldiers, are questionable, if not reprehensible means for governing them.

483. It is rare, indeed, that the practice of summary chastisement indulged in by some orderly sergeants with the unruly characters that are to be found in almost every company, can be regarded as successful. Individual instances, however, exist of very good government where the sergeant rules almost exclusively by physical force; but good judgment in forbearing to a point where the offender has placed himself beyond the consideration of kindness by his conduct, will be found to be the true secret of success in a physical-force policy.

484. Constantly present with the company, always on hand for every emergency, ever consulting the interests of the men and encouraging them in their duties, he cannot fail to attach them to the company, and make them cheerful and content, and faithful on duty.

REGIMENTAL HOSPITAL STEWARDS.

485. THE duties of hospital stewards of regiments do not differ materially from those of general or post hospitals. They occupy a similar position in the regimental hospitals; and their duties are only varied by the accidents of field service, which require them to be more active, as they have fewer

means and conveniences for the performance of their duties.

486. They receive the same pay and allowances as stewards of general hospitals, and are appointed by the commanding officer of the regiment, on the recommendation of the senior surgeon on duty in the regiment. When thus appointed, they can be reduced like other non-commissioned officers.

487. The legal organization of the old regiments does not allow of hospital stewards; but the new regiment of artillery is allowed one, and the new regiments of infantry are each entitled to three, called Battalion Hospital Stewards; whilst the regiments of artillery and infantry in the volunteer service are each allowed one, and the cavalry regiments of volunteers and regulars are each allowed two.

488. Hospital stewards in the volunteer service, when originally mustered in as such, cannot be reduced to the ranks, but may be dishonorably discharged. If promoted from the ranks, they may be reduced like other non-commissioned officers.

489. Those regiments of the old army that are not allowed hospital stewards by law can have them assigned from the Surgeon-General's Office.

490. In garrison there is little difference between the duties of a regimental steward, and those of a steward of a general or post hospital; but in the field his labors are materially varied, his attention being divided between the care and transportation

of the sick and that of the hospital property and medicines.

491. The hospitals in the field are more or less temporary, where the seriously sick and wounded are taken care of until they can be sent to the general hospitals; and slight cases only are treated for recovery. The means and material are necessarily limited: often it is only a tent or vacant building, and, in time of battle, the shade of trees, a ravine, or the shelter of a friendly wall.

492. The Hospital Department supplies a few stretchers, and the quartermaster a few ambulances and wagons, in which are a tent or two, medicines and instruments, and a mess-chest; and with these the attendants, and, in emergencies, the musicians, under the direction of the hospital steward, must do the best they can.

493. In tents the patients should be provided with bunks, and raised from the ground, as soon as possible. This may be done in numerous ways, particularly in a timbered country, and is advisable even for the most temporary hospitals. Much attention is required to keep the property of a field hospital in order, to protect it against great wear and tear.

494. Here the steward's agency is particularly required, and upon him depend that system and order that are so necessary to efficiency. He should see that every thing is in its place, properly stowed

away and in a condition for immediate use, and that deficiencies are made good at the earliest possible moment.

COMMISSARY SERGEANT.

495. THERE are two kinds of commissary sergeants,—regimental and company. The battalion commissary sergeants allowed to the new regiments of infantry have similar duties to those of regimental commissary sergeant.

496. The old regiments of artillery and infantry are not allowed commissary sergeants in their legal organization; and the duty is performed either by the quartermaster sergeant, or a sergeant detailed on extra duty for the purpose. All other regiments are allowed a commissary sergeant each.

497. He is appointed by the commanding officer of the regiment, on the recommendation of the regimental commissary, and receives the same pay as the quartermaster sergeant, twenty-two dollars per month, with an allowance of clothing and one ration. He is mustered and paid on the field and staff roll, and is under the direction of the regimental commissary, from whom he gets his instructions.

498. He has the immediate control of the commissary store-house, and receives and superintends the issues to the companies. He assists the clerk in

making up the returns, or may do the duties of clerk himself where the issues are not numerous.

499. Where the issues are frequent and large, he has more the duties of a foreman to perform, as he will have a great number of men under his direction. Where the beef is butchered by the commissary, the care of the cattle and the slaughtering involves an increased force that will also be under his direction.

500. The duty is a responsible one. Much property of a kind calculated to tempt the cupidity of a dishonest man is placed in his charge; and, even where the sergeant himself is strictly honest in the discharge of his duties, he is under the necessity of watching the employees, who frequently take opportunities of disposing of provisions for money or appropriating articles which they are not allowed to their own use. Frequent inspections are, therefore, necessary, to see that no deficiencies occur in this way.

501. Those men who have charge of particular issues should be held responsible for all deficiencies and be required to account for losses. Consequently, when a man is placed in charge of stores, a memorandum should be made of the amount, so that at any time that an inspection is made it may be correctly ascertained what should be on hand.

502. The commissary sergeant should keep an account of all receipts and issues daily. Then, if the stores are systematically stored, there is no diffi-

culty in making an inventory of them at any time, and correcting or discovering any delinquencies. Unless great vigilance is kept up, and a correct system pursued, deficiencies are sure to occur.

503. Some complication arises in returning for subsistence stores which are temporarily left in the commissary store,—as where companies leave their savings. In such cases, memorandum receipts should be given, and also an account of it should be kept; but at the end of each month every account should be squared up.

504. Issues are usually made to companies for ten days in garrisons or permanent camps, and for five days or less on the march. Consolidated returns should be made, as they save a multiplicity of papers. Each company renders a return, and they are consolidated in the adjutant's office and signed by the commanding officer.

The annexed miscellaneous items and tables are taken from the Regulations, and introduced to facilitate the duties and to assist in making issues and computations.

MISCELLANEOUS ITEMS.

1. When practicable, each kind of subsistence stores shall be placed by itself,—the packages stored so as to allow circulation among them, and to permit the quantity and age (date of purchase) of each lot being easily ascertained. At short intervals of time the stores and packages shall be carefully examined, and, when neces-

sary, separated for inspection, early issue, repacking, rebrining, &c., as circumstances may require.

2. When there is no flooring under stores, they must be placed on skids, or be otherwise properly dunnaged.

3. Salt meats in barrels should be piled *in tiers* only when limited store-room makes such storage necessary, and then never more than three tiers high, each tier resting on skids placed near the ends of the barrels.

4. Salt meats in pickle are not safe from injury unless there is undissolved salt in the barrel. The barrels should be rolled over monthly, and never be exposed to a hot sun.

5. Most subsistence stores being readily perishable, unremitting care is indispensable to their preservation.

6. The second chime-hoop on all barrels of pickled meats should be of iron. Two iron hoops on a barrel (one on each end) will generally be sufficient.

7. Vinegar-kegs should be painted, and the bungs capped with tin.

8. Liquid measures and scoops should be made of treble X tin.

9. The size, form, strength, &c. of packages designed to hold subsistence stores will be determined by the purchasing commissary, who will be governed in these particulars by the kind of transportation offered, by the size of the wagons used, by the convenience of handling the packages, &c.

10. When hard bread is put in boxes (the best packages for *field* transportation), they should be made of fully-seasoned wood, of a kind to impart no taste or odor to the bread, and as far as practicable of *single* pieces. When two pieces are used in making the same surface, they should be tongued and grooved together.

11. A box 26 x 17 x 11 inches, exterior measure, is an

average box for pilot bread, under the usual circumstances of land transportation. The ends of a box of this size should be made of inch, and the remainder of five-eighths, stuff, the package well strapped with green hickory or other suitable wood.

12. Hard bread, after *thorough* cooling and drying, should be pressed closely in its packages, each package containing a uniform weight *of bread*, for the convenience of calculation. It can be re-dried in boxes without removal therefrom, by being exposed for about forty hours to a temperature of 140 degrees Fahrenheit.

13. The army wagon being 22 x 42 x 114 inches, inside measurement, boxes for bacon made 20 x 20 x 28 inches outside measurement (which will contain 225 pounds of bacon) are convenient for *field* transportation. The boxes should be strapped, and the material be one and one-fourth inch thick, tongued and grooved.

14. A box, 4 x 4 inches square, and 3.6 inches deep, will contain one quart, or 57.75 cubic inches.

15. A box, 5 x 5 inches square, and 4.6 inches deep, will contain a half-gallon, or 115.5 cubic inches.

16. A box, 24 x 16 inches square, and 28 inches deep, will contain one barrel (large whisky barrel), or 10,752 cubic inches.

17. A box, 8 x 8.4 inches square, and 8 inches deep, will contain one peck, or 537.6 cubic inches.

18. A box, 16 x 16.8 inches square, and 8 inches deep, will contain one bushel, or 2150 cubic inches.

Rate per bushel at which certain cereals, esculent roots, &c. shall be estimated.

One bushel of corn (on the cob) at		. . . .	70 pounds.
"	"	corn (shelled)	"	56 "
"	"	corn meal	"	50 "
"	"	hominy	"	45 "
"	"	rye	"	56 "
"	"	buckwheat	"	52 "
"	"	barley		
"	"	wheat		
"	"	beans		
"	"	peas		
"	"	onions		
"	"	beets	"	60 "
"	"	carrots		
"	"	turnips		
"	"	potatoes		
"	"	fine salt		
"	"	bran	"	20 "
"	"	malt	"	38 "
"	"	dried apples	"	24 "
"	"	dried peaches		
"	"	oats	"	32 "

Schedule of tares prescribed by the Treasury Department for the government of the collectors of customs and others interested.

Cheese, 10 per cent. for casks or tubs.

Coffee, Rio, 1 per cent. 8ingle bags; 2 per cent., double bags. All other coffee, actual tare.

Cocoa, 2 per cent., bags; 8 per cent., ceroons.

Chicory, 2 per cent., bags.

Melado, 11 per cent.

Pepper, 2 per cent., bags; 4 per cent., double bags.

Pimento, 2 per cent., bags.

Rice, 2 per cent., bags.

Sugar, 12 1/2 per cent. for hogshead; 12 per cent. for tierces; 10 per cent., barrels; 14 per cent., boxes; 2 per cent., bags; 2 1/2 per cent., mats.

Salt, fine, in sacks, 3 pounds for each sack. Coarse or ground alum, 2 pounds each.

Teas, duty to be levied on the net number of pounds, as per invoice, when from China or Japan.

All others, actual tare by weight.

Table showing the Weight and Bulk of 1,000 Rations.*

1,000 Rations.	Net weight, lbs.	Gross weight, lbs.	Bulk in barrels.
Pork	750	1,253	4.6
Bacon	750	883	4.5333
Salt beef	1,250	2,239	7.6666
Flour	1,375	1,507	7.0153
Hard bread, in barrels	1,000	1,211	11.1111
Hard bread, in boxes	1,000	1,262	9.6
Beans and peas	159	162	.6666
Rice and hominy	100	108	.5188
Coffee, green	100	122	.6453
Coffee, roasted	80	108	.8326
Coffee, ground	80	102	.7592
Tea	15	19	.16
Sugar	150	161	.6
Vinegar	80	97	.4121
Candles, adamantine	12 1/2	16 1/2	.08888
Soap	40	44	.14
Salt	37 1/2	40 1/2	.1402
Pepper	2 1/2	4	.3466
Potatoes, fresh	300	345	.18285
Molasses	32 1/2	34 1/3	.1133
Desiccated potatoes	93 3/4	116 3/4	.7708
Desiccated vegetables	62 1/2	75 1/2	.4342
Whiskey	77 1/2	91 1/2	.4043
1,000 complete rations†	3,031.09	3,885.6	19.1218
1 complete ration	3.03	3.88	
1,000 complete rations‡	2,543.58	3,418.08	18.5857
1 complete ration	2.54	3.41	
1,000 complete rations§	2,918.58	3,663.08	16.
1 complete ration	2.91	3.66	

* This table is constructed upon the basis of a ration as allowed during the war and as ordinarily put up for transportation. The weight (net and gross) and bulk of 1,000 rations will, of course, vary with the component parts put up, and with the kind of package used. In calculating the *bulk* of Subsistence Stores for purposes of storage or transportation, six and one fourth (6 1/4) cubic feet are considered a *barrel*.

† Consisting of 1/2 pork, 1/4 salt beef, 1/4 bacon; 1/2 flour, 1/2 bread, in boxes; beans or peas; rice or hominy; 3/4 roasted and ground coffee, 1/4 tea; sugar; vinegar; adamantine candles; soap; salt; pepper; molasses; potatoes.

‡ Consisting of 1/2 pork, 1/4 salt beef, 1/4 bacon; bread in boxes; beans or peas; rice or hominy; 3/4 roasted and ground coffee, 1/4 tea; sugar; vinegar; adamantine candles; soap; salt; pepper; molasses.

§ Consisting of 1/2 pork, 1/4 salt beef, 1/4 bacon; flour; beans or peas; rice or hominy; 3/4 roasted and ground coffee, 1/4 tea; sugar; vinegar; adamantine candles; soap; salt; pepper; molasses.

Table showing the Quantity and Bulk of any Number of Rations, from 1 to 100,000.

NUMBER OF RATIONS.	PORK, BACON-SIDES, SHOULDERS, HAMS, ETC.		BEEF, SALT AND FRESH, AND CORN MEAL.		FLOUR AND SOFT BREAD.		BEANS, PEAS, AND SUGAR.*		RICE, HOMINY, AND GREEN COFFEE.		ROASTED COFFEE.	
	Pounds.	Ounces.	Pounds.	Ounces.	Pounds.	Ounces.	Pounds.	Ounces.	Pounds.	Ounces.	Pounds.	Ounces.
1	....	12	1	4	1	6	......	2.4	....	1.6	....	1.28
2	1	8	2	8	2	12	......	4.8	....	3.2	....	2.56
3	2	4	3	12	4	2	......	7.2	....	4.8	....	3.84
4	3	..	5	..	5	8	......	9.6	....	6.4	....	5.12
5	3	12	6	4	6	14	......	12.0	....	8.0	....	6.4
6	4	8	7	8	8	4	......	14.4	....	9.6	....	7.68
7	5	4	8	12	9	10	1	0.8	....	11.2	....	8.96
8	6	..	10	..	11	..	1	3.2	....	12.8	....	10.24
9	6	12	11	4	12	6	1	5.6	....	14.4	....	11.52
10	7	8	12	8	13	12	1	8.0	1	..	....	12.8
20	15	..	25	..	27	8	8	..	2	..	1	9.6
30	22	8	37	8	41	4	4	8.0	3	..	2	6.4
40	3	..	50	..	55	..	6	..	4	..	3	3.2
50	37	8	62	8	68	12	7	8.0	5	..	4	..
60	45	..	75	..	82	8	9	..	6	..	4	12.8
70	52	8	87	8	96	4	10	8.0	7	..	5	..
80	60	..	100	..	110	..	12	..	8	..	6	..
90	67	8	112	8	123	12	13	8.0	9	..	7	3.2
100	75	..	125	..	137	8	15	..	10	..	8	..
200	150	..	250	..	275	..	30	..	20	..	16	..
300	225	..	375	..	412	8	45	..	30	..	21	..
400	300	..	500	..	550	..	60	..	40	..	32	..
500	375	..	625	..	687	8	75	..	50	..	40	..
600	450	..	750	..	825	..	90	..	60	..	48	..
700	525	..	375	..	962	8	105	..	70	..	56	..
800	600	..	1,000	..	1,100	..	120	..	80	..	64	..
900	675	..	1,125	..	1,237	8	135	..	90	..	72	..
1,000	750	..	1,250	..	1,375	..	150	..	100	..	80	..
5,000	3,750	..	6,250	..	6,875	..	750	..	500	..	400	..
10,000	7,500	..	12,500	..	13,750	..	1,500	..	1,000	..	800	..
50,000	37,500	..	62,500	..	68,750	..	7,500	..	5,000	..	4,000	..
100,000	75,000	..	125,000	..	137,500	..	15,000	..	10,000	..	8,000	..

* Beans, peas, salt, and potatoes (fresh) shall be purchased, issued, and sold by weight, and the *bushel* of each shall be estimated at *sixty pounds*.

† *Roasted and ground* coffee is issued at the same rate as roasted coffee.

NOTES.—Fresh onions, beets, carrots, and turnips, when on hand, may be issued *in lieu* of beans, peas, rice, or hominy, and at the rate of potatoes (fresh), viz.: thirty pounds to 100 rations.

Dried apples, dried peaches, pickles, &c., when on hand, may be issued *in lieu* of any component part of the ration, of equal money value.

Table showing the Quantity and Bulk of any Number of Rations,
from 1 to 100,000.
Continued.

NUMBER OF RATIONS.	TEA.		VINEGAR.			CANDLES, ADAMANTINE OR STAR.		SOAP.		SALT.	
	Pounds.	Ounces.	Gallons.	Quarts.	Gills.	Pounds.	Ounces.	Pounds.	Ounces.	Pounds.	Ounces.
1		0.24			0.32		0.2		0.64		0.6
2		0.48			0.61		0.4		1.28		1.2
3		0.72			0.96		0.6		1.92		1.8
4		0.96			1.28		0.8		2.56		2.4
5		1.2			1.6		1.		3.2		3.
6		1.44			1.92		1.2		3.84		3.6
7		1.68			2.24		1.4		4.48		4.2
8		1.92			2.56		1.6		5.12		4.8
9		2.16			2.88		1.8		5.76		5.4
10		2.4			3.2		2.		6.4		6.
20		4.8			6.4		4.		12.8		12.
30		7.2		1	1.6		6.	1	3.2	1	2.
40		9.6		1	4.8		8.	1	9.6	1	8.
50		12.0		2			10.	2		1	14.
60		14.4		2	3.2		12.	2	6.4	2	4.
70	1	0.8		2	6.4		14.	2	12.8	2	10.
80	1	3.2		3	1.6	1		3	3.2	3	
90	1	5.6		3	4.8	1	2.	3	9.6	3	6.
100	1	8.	1			1	4.	4		3	12.
200	3		2			2	8.	8		7	8.
300	4	8.	3			3	12.	12		11	4.
400	6		4			5		16		15	
500	7	8.	5			6	4.	20		18	12.
600	9		6			7	8.	24		22	8.
700	10	8.	7			8	12.	28		26	4.
800	12		8			10		32		30	
900	13	8.	9			11	4.	36		33	12.
1,000	15		10			12	8.	40		37	8.
5,000	75		50			62	8.	200		187	8.
10,000	150		100			125		400		375	
50,000	750		500			625		2,000		1,875	
100,000	1,500		1,000			1,250		4,000		3,750	

Table showing the Quantity and Bulk of any Number of Rations,
from 1 to 100,000.
Concluded.

NUMBER OF RATIONS.	PEPPER.		POTATOES.*		MOLASSES.			DESICCATED POTATOES.		MIXED VEGETABLES.	
	Pounds.	Ounces.	Pounds.	Ounces.	Gallons.	Quarts.	Gills.	Pounds.	Ounces.	Pounds.	Ounces.
1	....	.04	....	4.8	....	....	0.08	....	1.5	....	1
2	....	.08	....	9.6	....	....	0.16	....	3.	....	2
3	....	.12	....	14.4	....	....	0.24	....	4.5	....	3
4	....	.16	1	3.2	....	....	0.32	....	6.	....	4
5	....	.20	1	8.	....	....	0.40	....	7.5	....	5
6	....	.24	1	12.8	....	....	0.48	....	9.	....	6
7	....	.28	2	1.6	....	....	0.56	....	10.5	....	7
8	....	.32	2	6.4	....	....	0.64	....	12.	....	8
9	....	.36	2	11.2	....	....	0.72	....	13.5	....	9
10	....	.40	3	....	....	....	0.80	....	15.	....	10
20	....	.80	6	....	....	....	1.60	1	14.	1	4
30	....	1.2	9	....	....	....	2.40	2	13.	1	14
40	....	1.6	12	....	....	....	3.20	3	12.	2	8
50	....	2.	15	....	....	....	4.	4	11.	3	2
60	....	2.4	17	....	....	....	4.8	5	10.	3	12
70	....	2.8	21	....	....	....	5.6	6	9.	4	6
80	....	3.2	21	....	....	....	6.4	7	8.	5	....
90	....	3.6	27	....	....	....	7.2	8	7.	5	10
100	....	4.	30	....	....	1	....	9	6.	6	4
200	....	8.	60	....	....	2	....	18	12.	12	8
300	....	12.	90	....	....	3	....	28	2.	18	12
400	1	....	120	....	1	....	....	37	8.	25	....
500	1	4.	150	....	1	1	....	46	14.	31	4
600	1	8.	180	....	1	2	....	56	4.	37	8
700	1	12.	210	....	1	3	....	65	10.	43	12
800	2	....	240	....	2	....	....	75	....	50	....
900	2	4.	270	....	2	1	....	84	6.	56	4
1,000	2	8.	300	....	2	2	....	93	12.	62	8
5,000	12	8.	1,500	....	12	2	....	468	12.	312	8
10,000	25	....	3,000	....	25	....	....	937	8.	625	....
50,000	125	....	15,000	....	125	....	....	4,687	8.	3,125	....
100,000	250	....	30,000	....	250	....	....	9,375	....	6,250	....

* Beans, peas, salt, and potatoes (fresh) shall be purchased, issued, and sold by weight, and the *bushel* of each shall be estimated at *sixty pounds*.

505. The sergeant should be thoroughly acquainted with the regulations for the subsistence department; otherwise he cannot superintend the details of his office with confidence. The care of the stores requires simply common sense, and a practical knowledge of the properties of the various articles issued as subsistence stores for the army, and the causes that usually produce deterioration; also, the means usually adopted to prevent stores from spoiling and to keep them in the best possible state of preservation.

506. There is little difference between the field and garrison duties of a commissary sergeant. In the field, he has the stores in charge the same as in garrison, receives and issues them, but has a more limited means of taking care of them, and, consequently, rarely has more on hand than is absolutely necessary.

507. The commissary department furnishes scales, weights, and measures, which he should always keep on hand; for without them he will be unable to give satisfaction to the troops without running the risk of exceeding the authorized issues.

508. As the quartermaster takes charge of the transportation of the stores, they are necessarily, whilst in his charge and in transit, out of the control of the commissary department for the time-being; but it is the sergeant's duty to note the amount he turns over for transportation, to give invoices and take transportation receipts.

509. These should be signed by the quartermaster and commissary. In regiments where the quartermaster is also commissary, this is not necessary, and he simply co-operates with the quartermaster sergeant, the latter attending immediately to the teams or means of transport, and the former looking after the stores.

THE COMPANY COMMISSARY SERGEANT.

510. THIS office is of recent date, and is authorized only in the mounted regiments and the new artillery regiment. The same pay and allowances are authorized as for company quartermaster sergeants. He is, however, only a part of the company organization, and under the direction of the company commander.

511. His duty is to make out the provision return, attend to drawing the rations for the company, and superintend their cooking and distribution to the men. He takes care of the company savings, and keeps the account with the commissary.

512. He is required to know the drill, and attends the exercises the same as other non-commissioned officers, except where they would interfere with the performance of his legitimate duties. He should also be familiar with all that has been prescribed for the duty-sergeants of the company.

513. The utmost impartiality should be exercised by the sergeant in the distribution of the provi-

sions, to prevent discontent among the men. They should all be served alike, as far as it is possible. Close attention is necessary in the care of the stores; and none of the men should be permitted to help themselves. No one except the cooks should have access to the provisions, and these only when the sergeant is present.

514. The provisions for one meal only should be issued to them at one time to be cooked; and when they are ready for issue, the sergeant should be present, and see that they are equitably distributed and that the proper allowance is saved for those who are necessarily absent, that the prisoners are supplied, and also all others who are entitled to rations from the company.

THE QUARTERMASTER SERGEANT.

515. A REGIMENTAL quartermaster sergeant is allowed to each regiment or battalion in the army. A quartermaster sergeant is also allowed to each company in the cavalry and in the Fifth Artillery. The former belongs to the non-commissioned staff, and the latter is mustered on the company rolls next below the first sergeant. They both receive the same pay and allowances,—regimental and company quartermaster sergeants,—viz.: twenty-two dollars per month, an allowance of clothing, and one ration.

516. The quartermaster sergeant of the regiment

is appointed by the regimental commander, on the recommendation of the quartermaster of the regiment, and should be exclusively under the orders of the latter; and all orders the sergeant has to execute should properly be transmitted through his chief. Should he receive orders from any other officer, he should report the orders to his chief, who will either approve or assume the responsibility of disobeying the orders.

517. The duties of this sergeant are to take the immediate charge of the property for which the regimental quartermaster is responsible, and direct the employees and the details sent to work for the quartermaster department. He receives and takes note of the stores received, and makes the issues authorized by the quartermaster. It is a responsible duty, and requires great industry, energy and activity, but above all integrity; as there is much temptation to misapply public property.

518. The duties are more extensive and responsible than those of the commissary sergeant, he has more men under his direction, usually, and a greater amount and variety of property in charge; and, as the property is generally in use and scattered in every direction throughout the regiment, the utmost attention is necessary to prevent loss.

519. It is difficult to lay down detailed instructions on the duties of sergeants, where each quartermaster has his own way of requiring the duty to be done. In a regiment, however, some uniformity

of practice might be established that would be a guide for all.

520. In the evening, between retreat and tattoo, the sergeant should report to the quartermaster how he has succeeded in the performance of the duties of the day, and receive his instructions for the morrow. He, being the foreman of all the workmen, teamsters, laborers, &c., employed by the quartermaster in the regiment, should receive all the orders, and, if necessary, have assistants to aid him.

521. He generally has a wagon-master in charge of the regimental train under his direction. When details report for work, there is usually a non-commissioned officer in charge of them, to whom he can look for assistance in carrying out orders. Regimental quartermasters rarely are authorized to employ citizens: all the aid he requires is usually furnished from the companies of the regiment, on proper application, and the labors of these men are usually under the direction of the quartermaster sergeant.

522. The attention of the sergeant is more important on some matters of property than others. Clothing, camp and garrison equipage, being only for issue to the troops, require the utmost care, as each particular article is invoiced, and must be accounted for, or else paid for by the quartermaster. Deficiencies in this kind of property are difficult to

account for; and it is necessary to be absolutely accurate in keeping the account of it.

523. All property must be accounted for; but losses and deficiencies of other property are more easily explained away than with clothing, camp and garrison equipage. Articles worn out and unserviceable should be carefully preserved until they have been inspected, condemned, and ordered to be dropped.

524. When property is lost or destroyed, the sergeant should be careful to get the certificates of officers, or the affidavit of citizens or soldiers, giving the circumstances of the loss.

525. Property transferred should be invoiced at once, and receipts obtained. In this respect the utmost promptness is necessary; and it should never be put off until to-morrow if it can possibly be done to-day.

526. In all matters in the quartermaster's department, but particularly in the papers, there should be no postponement of any thing, if it can be done at once; otherwise, besides accumulating a mountain of unfinished labor, much of it never can be done, because the opportunity has been permitted to pass when it might have been done.

527. Thus, if an officer does not give his receipt at the proper time to the quartermaster, it will be impossible to tell whether he will ever get it; for he may be ordered away, he may get killed in the

morrow's fight, be discharged or dismissed from service, or the same may happen to the quartermaster.

528. In cavalry and artillery regiments, the procuring and distribution of forage is the heaviest item of the quartermaster sergeant's duties, and requires great attention; and the wants of the troops should always be anticipated.

529. In the field, where the forage is obtained from the surrounding country, the sergeant or other person in charge of forage-parties should give receipts to the person furnishing the forage, instructing him to present the receipt to the quartermaster as soon as possible and obtain his pay or a certified voucher; for, if the troops move, the man may have great difficulty in getting his pay.

530. Regiments of infantry also require a certain amount of forage for the regimental teams and the field-officers' horses, that is procured in the same way. The accounts of all issues of forage should be faithfully kept, particularly when, as is the case on the march, the issues are made daily. The requisitions and receipts for forage should be promptly collected at the end of each month.

531. Providing fuel for the troops, especially in the winter season, is also an important duty generally intrusted to the quartermaster sergeant, and requires the same attention and punctuality as forage.

THE COMPANY QUARTERMASTER SERGEANT.

532. THE quartermaster sergeant of the company performs the same duties with reference to the company that the regimental sergeant does towards the regiment. He is under the direction of the company commander and first sergeant.

533. He receives the fuel and forage for the company from the quartermaster sergeant, and keeps the account. He takes charge of the wagon assigned to the company, and all the company property in it. In garrison he has the immediate charge of the company store-room.

534. He attends to receiving the clothing, camp and garrison equipage, and assists the first sergeant in its distribution. He also receives all other quartermaster's property turned over to the company, and sees that it is properly cared for, and must be able to account for it to his company commander.

535. On the march, he attends to the loading and unloading of the wagons, and superintends the erection of tents, putting up the picket-line, &c. He sees that the forage is properly distributed and that the public animals are fed.

536. He should be able to identify all the animals belonging to the company; he reports their wants and necessities to the company commander; he sees that they are properly cared for by the men,

and that the sick horses are reported to the veterinary surgeon for treatment.

537. He procures the fuel for the company, makes out the requisitions for the company commander to sign, and draws the fuel from the quartermaster sergeant.

538. Straw for bedding for men and horses is procured in the same way.

539. He keeps the register of the camp and garrison equipage issued to the men of the company, and such other quartermaster's property as may be intrusted to them.

540. Like the commissary sergeant of the company, he should be familiar with the drill and other duties of the company sergeants, and, when necessary, may be required in the ranks to perform his part in times of danger. Usually, however, at such times his presence is more necessary to look out for the safety of the company property.

NOTE.—In what has been stated with regard to the duty of the first sergeant, the quartermaster and commissary sergeants of the company, concerning the making out of certain papers, requisitions, provision returns, &c., it is not necessarily meant that they shall make out these papers themselves; the company clerk usually does it under their direction; but they should at least be able to do it in case of necessity from any cause.

THE SERGEANT MAJOR.

541. THE sergeant major is the ranking non-commissioned officer of the regiment: he is appointed by the regimental commander. Each regiment in service is entitled to one sergeant major, and the nine new regiments of infantry are allowed one to each battalion. His pay is twenty-six dollars per month, an allowance of clothing, and one ration.

542. The sergeant major assists the adjutant in the performance of his duties; he makes the details for guard, fatigue, &c. under his direction, parades them, verifies the number required from each company, and sees that they are properly equipped for the duty for which they have been detailed.

543. He superintends the clerk, and assists him in making out the various returns, rolls, and reports required, and in keeping the books and records of the regiment.

544. He keeps the roster of the sergeants and corporals and of the various details for guard, fatigue, detachments, &c., and is responsible that these duties are equally required from the various companies.

545. He generally keeps the time at head-quarters, and sees that the musician detailed for the purpose at head-quarters sounds the calls at the proper time.

546. At orderly call, he returns the morning report books to the first sergeants, gives them the orders for the day, and furnishes them with the details required from their respective companies for the morrow. The orders, to be copied in the company order-book, are also furnished them.

547. In the absence of a drum-major or principal musician, the musicians of the companies are controlled and directed by him, and he attends to their instruction. He sees that they attend practice, and that they do not absent themselves without authority.

548. He keeps their roster for the various duties of orderly, guard, fatigue, &c. Should there be a regimental band and no authorized leader or drum-major, he performs a similar duty as in the case of company musicians.

549. The sergeant major attends at guard-mounting, taking post in front and on the right of the line on which the guard is to form, facing to the left. As each first sergeant marches his detail upon the line, and having brought it "*to rear open order*," and "*right dress*," he receives the report from the first sergeants, "all present," or, so many sergeants, corporals, or privates "absent." He then verifies the reports of the first sergeants, after which the sergeant major brings his sword to a "present," and reports, "*Sir, the guard is formed, all present*," or, so many sergeants, corporals, and privates "absent." The adjutant then gives the

command "*front*," and the sergeant major takes post two paces on the left of the guard, and the guard, mounting, then proceeds as prescribed in Regulations.

550. At dress-parade, the sergeant major posts the left guide or marker, and, after all the companies have formed, he takes his post two paces on the extreme left of the regiment. When the guard or regiment marches in review, the sergeant marches on the left of the guard or rear platoon, two paces, or on the left of the rear company or platoon.

551. The sergeant major should be a model soldier for the rest of the regiment in his dress and military deportment. His example and punctual requirements of duty go far towards influencing a proper discipline in the regiment. If a due regard for the merits of the non-commissioned officers of the regiment is maintained, he will be the first to succeed to a commission in the regiment.

THE CADET.

552. THE United States Military Academy is located on the west bank of the Hudson River, about fifty miles from New York City. It is maintained and supported at the Government expense, and is under the direction of the Chief of the Engineer Corps. The superintendent is an officer selected from the Engineer Corps, with the local rank

of colonel. The commandant is taken from the line of the army, with the local rank of lieutenant colonel. The professors of the different branches are permanently located at the Academy. The superintendent, commandant, assistant professors, and instructors are taken from the officers of the regular army, and continue on duty at the discretion of the War Department. It is, however, the custom to relieve them, at the end of four years' service, by other officers.

553. The students, called cadets, are appointed by the Secretary of War, on the nomination of the member of Congress of the district or the delegate from the Territory from which the cadet is appointed. Each Congressional district or Territory, and the District of Columbia, is entitled to a representative. The President is authorized to appoint ten at large, without reference to districts; and he also makes the appointment for the District of Columbia.

554. The appointments at large are generally given to the sons of distinguished officers of the army and navy who have been killed or died in service. This rule is, however, not implicitly observed.

555. Candidates are required to be between the ages of sixteen and twenty-one years, physically sound, and of good moral character and habits. They are allowed the same pay as the Naval Cadets, which is five hundred dollars per year (Act April 1, 1864, sec. 3,) out of which all expenses are paid for

clothing, books, board, lights, washing, and other incidental expenses. They are not allowed to draw the money; but on leaving the Academy, the balance, after deducting all expenses, is paid them.

556. The appointments are usually made in March, and the cadet is required to report at the Academy between the 1st and 20th of June. Before he is admitted, the cadet undergoes a rigid medical examination of his physical qualifications, and also as to his proficiency in reading, writing, the four ground-rules of arithmetic, reduction, and vulgar and decimal fractions.

557. Cadets reporting before the 20th of June have the advantage of the intermediate time to prepare themselves for the preliminary examination under the instruction of some older cadets selected for the purpose, which familiarizes them with the manner of recitation and instruction and gives them a foretaste of what their academic life is likely to be. By reporting early, the cadet may save himself the mortification of being rejected.

558. Vacancies occurring after the 1st of July and before the 1st of September are filled, if in time to report on or before the 1st of September. Cadets appointed during this interval are at some disadvantage with their class-mates, on account of entering three months later.

559. At the end of two years, if the conduct of the cadet has been sufficiently good, he receives a

furlough from after the June examination until the 28th of August. If he has been economical, he will have saved some money, which is paid him to assist him in going on furlough.

560. About forty cadets graduate annually, being a little more than one-third of those appointed. On graduating, the cadet receives a leave of absence until the 1st of October. The graduation takes place about the 25th of June. In the mean time an order is published from the War Department assigning the graduates to corps and regiments, according to standing.

561. Not much choice is allowed the graduates. Formerly, before the increase of the army, they were generally assigned according to class-rank, ordinarily Nos. 1 and 2 to the engineer corps, Nos. 3 and 4 to the topographical engineers, Nos. 5 and 6 to the ordnance corps, Nos. 7 to 20 to the artillery regiments, and the remainder to the infantry and cavalry regiments. As the prospects of promotion affected the assignments, the highest on the class-roll receiving the assignment that promised the speediest promotion, there was no great room for preference.

562. If there were no vacancies in the different regiments, the graduates were assigned as supernumerary officers, with the lowest rank (brevet second lieutenant), not to exceed one to each company. Since the increase of the army, however, the number of graduates annually is not sufficient

to fill the vacancies that occur; and the remainder have been filled from the army or from civil life.

563. The regulations of the Academy are very strict, and are rigidly enforced. Patience, perseverance, and industry are the principal qualities necessary to accomplish the course, as it is not beyond the capacity of the majority of young men. Method, unremitting application, and fondness for the cadet life seem necessary to enable one to pass through it successfully.

564. It will not do to become disgusted or discouraged; and the cadet should avoid the error of thinking that he is the object of a petty malevolence on the part of any of the professors or instructors, as instances of such injustice are extremely rare; and such thoughts should not be indulged in without the most satisfactory proofs, which would readily obtain redress when made known to the superintendent or commandant.

565. The following circular can be obtained by applicants by addressing the Chief of the Engineer Corps, Washington, D. C.

REGULATIONS

RELATIVE TO THE ADMISSION OF CADETS INTO THE MILITARY ACADEMY.

As frequent inquiries are made in regard to the mode of procuring admission into the Military Academy, all persons interested in the subject are hereby informed that applications should be made by letter to the Secretary of War. By provision of law, each Congressional and Territorial district, and the District of Columbia, is entitled to have one cadet at the Military Academy, and no more. The district appointments are made on the nomination of the member of Congress representing the district at the date of the appointment. The law requires that the individual selected shall be an actual resident of the Congressional district of the State or Territory, or District of Columbia, from which the appointment purports to be made. Also appointments "at large," not to exceed ten, are annually made. Application can be made, at any time, by the candidate himself, his parent, guardian, or any of his friends, and the name placed on the register. No preference will be given to applications on account of priority; nor will any application be entered in the register when the candidate is under or above the prescribed age; the *precise age* must be given; *no relaxation of the regulation in this respect will be made*; nor will any application be considered in cases where the age and other qualifications of the candidates are not stated. The fixed abode of the candidate, and *number* of the Congressional district which he considers his permanent residence, must be set forth in the application. The pay of a cadet is thirty dollars per month, to commence with his admission into the Military Academy, and is considered ample, with proper economy, for his support.

The appointments will be made annually in the month of February or March, on the applications made within the current or preceding year. The claims of all the candidates on the register will be considered and acted upon. No certain information can be given as to the probable success of the candidate before the arrival of the period for making the selections. Persons, therefore, making applications, must not expect to receive information on this point.

As a general rule, no person will be appointed who has had a brother educated at the institution.

QUALIFICATIONS.

Candidates must be over sixteen and under twenty-one years of age at the time of entrance into the Military Academy; must be at least five feet in height, and free from any deformity, disease, or infirmity which would render them unfit for the military service, and from any disorder of an infectious or immoral character. They must be able to read and write well, and perform with facility and accuracy the various operations of the four ground-rules of arithmetic, of reduction, of simple and compound proportion, and of vulgar and decimal fractions.

It must he understood that a full compliance with the above conditions will be insisted on—that is to say, the candidate must write in a fair and legible hand, and without any material mistakes in spelling, such sentences as shall be dictated by the examiners: and he must answer promptly, and without errors, all their questions in the above-mentioned rules of arithmetic: failing in any of these particulars, he will he rejected.

It must also be understood that every candidate will, soon after his arrival at West Point, be subjected to a rigid examination by an experienced medical board; and should there be found to exist in him any of the following causes of disqualification to such a degree as will immediately, or in all probability may at no very distant period, impair his efficiency, he will be rejected:—

1. Feeble constitution and muscular tenuity; unsound

health, from whatever cause; indications of former disease; glandular swellings, or other symptoms of scrofula.

2. Chronic cutaneous affections, especially of the scalp, or of any disorder of an infectious character.

3. Severe injuries of the bones of the head; convulsions.

4. Impaired vision, from whatever cause; inflammatory affections of the eyelids; immobility or irregularity of the iris; fistula lachrymalis, &c. &c.

5. Deafness; copious discharge from the ears.

6. Loss of many teeth, or teeth generally unsound.

7. Impediment of speech.

8. Want of due capacity of the chest, and any other indication of a liability to pulmonic disease.

9. Impaired or inadequate efficiency of one or both of the superior extremities, on account of fractures, especially of the clavicle, contraction of a joint, extenuation, deformity, &c. &c.

10. An unnatural excurvature or incurvature of the spine.

11. Hernia.

12. A varicose state of the veins, of the scrotum and spermatic cord (when large), sarcocele, hydrocele, hemorrhoids, fistulas.

13. Impaired or inadequate efficiency of one or both of the inferior extremities on account of varicose veins, fractures, malformation (flat feet, &c.), lameness, contraction, unequal length, bunions, overlying or supernumerary toes, &c. &c.

14. Ulcers, or unsound cicatrices of ulcers likely to break out afresh.

SIMON CAMERON,

Secretary of War.

WAR DEPARTMENT, September 16, 1861.

The following is a synopsis of the course of studies pursued at the Military Academy:—

FIRST YEAR.

Fourth Class.

Mathematics.—Davies' Bourdon's Algebra; Davies' Legendre's Geometry and Trigonometry; Davies' Descriptive Geometry.

English Grammar, including Etymological and Rhetorical exercises; Composition, Declamation, and Geography of the United States.—Bullion's Grammar; Vocabularies and Exercises by Professor French; Morse's Geography; Sargent's Elocution; Parker's Aids to English Composition; Roget's Thesaurus of English Words; Worcester's Dictionary.

French.—Bolmar's Lévizae's Grammar; Bolmar's Verb Book; Agnel's Tabular System; Berard's Leçons Françaises; Chapsal's Leçons et Modèles de Littérature Française.

Use of Small Arms.—Instruction in Fencing and Bayonet Exercise.

SECOND YEAR.

Third Class.

Mathematics.—Davies' Descriptive Geometry; Davies' Shades, Shadows and Perspective; Davies' Spherical Projections and Warped Surfaces; Davies' Surveying; Church's Analytical Geometry; Church's Calculus.

French.—Bomar's Lévizae's Grammar; Bolmar's Verb Book; Agnel's Tabular System; Rowan's Morceaux Choisis des Auteurs Modernes.

Drawing.—Human Figure; Topography.

Cavalry.—Practical Instruction in Cavalry Exercise.

THIRD YEAR.
Second Class.

Natural and Experimental Philosophy.—Bartlett's Mechanics; Bartlett's Acoustics and Optics; Bartlett's Astronomy.

Chemistry.—Fowne's Chemistry; Electrics, from Miller's Physics of Chemistry.

Drawing.—Landscape.

Infantry Tactics.—Rules for the Exercise and Manœuvres of the United States Infantry; Jomini's Art of War.

Artillery Tactics.—Tactics for Garrison, Siege, and Field Artillery; Thackeray's Army Organization and Administration; Extracts from McClellan's Military Commission to Europe; Army Regulations.

Cavalry.—Practical Instruction in Cavalry Exercise.

FOURTH YEAR.
First Class.

Engineering, Civil and Military.—Mahan's Course of Civil Engineering; Mahan's Lithographic Notes on Stone-Cutting; Mahan's Lithographic Notes on Machines; Mahan's Treatise on Field Fortifications; Mahan's Lithographic Notes on Permanent Fortification; Attack and Defence; Mines and other Accessories; Mahan's Treatise on Advanced Guards and Outposts, &c.

Practical Engineering.—Practical Instruction in Fabricating Fascines, Sap-fagots, Gabions, Hurdles, Sap-rollers, &c.; Manner of laying out and constructing Gun and Mortar Batteries, Field Fortifications, and Works of Siege; formation of Stockades, Abatis, &c.; Topographical Sketching in the Field, embracing rapid methods of reconnoitring woods, heights, defiles, fields, marshes water-courses, fords, bridges, roads, and other communications, houses, villages, batteries, field-works, &c. &c.; Recitations upon Field Fortification, Sapping, Mining, Pontonniering, and Military Reconnoissance.

Ethics, Constitutional, International, and Military Law.—Kent's Commentaries; Practical Ethics by Professor French; De Hart on Courts-Martial; Preliminary Lecture on Law, by Professor French.

Mineralogy and Geology.—Dana's Mineralogy; Hitchcock's Geology.

Ordnance and Gunnery.—Practical Pyrotechny; Benton's Course of Instruction in Ordnance and Gunnery.

Spanish.—Josse's Grammar; Morales' Progressive Reader; Ollendorf's Oral Method, applied to the Spanish by Velasquez and Simmone.

Cavalry Tactics.—Cavalry Tactics for United States Service; Youatt on the Horse.

Cavalry.—Practical Instruction in Cavalry Exercise.

566. The first appointment is only a conditional one; and the cadet must pass the preliminary examinations, and the semi-annual examination in January following, before he can receive his warrant, which is then made out, to date from the 3d of June previous. At the time of receiving his warrant, the cadet takes the oath of allegiance to the United States, and that he will serve them honestly and faithfully for eight years from the date of his warrant, unless sooner discharged. The following section of the Act of August 3, 1861, requires the following oath to be taken on admission, viz.;—

"Sec. 8. *And be it further enacted*, That no cadet, who has been or shall hereafter be reported as deficient, either in conduct or studies, and recommended to be discharged from the Academy, shall be returned or reappointed, or appointed to any place in the army before his class shall have left the Academy and received their commissions, unless upon the recommendation of the academic board of the Academy: *Provided*, That all cadets now in the service, or hereafter entering the Military Academy at West Point, shall be called on to take and subscribe the following oath: 'I, A. B., do solemnly swear that I will support the Constitution of the United States, and bear true allegiance to the national government; that I will maintain and defend the sovereignty of the United States paramount to any and all allegiance, sovereignty, or fealty I may owe to any State, county, or country whatsoever; and that I will at all times obey the legal orders of my superior officers and the rules and articles governing the armies of the United States.' And any cadet or candidate for admission who shall refuse to take this oath shall be dismissed from the service."

567. During the months of July and August, all the cadets, except the second class, which is then on furlough, go into an encampment at the post, and are employed in military duties and exercises in the field until September. During this period they enjoy a relaxation from study; and, although they are quite busily employed, they still have good opportunities for pleasure and amusement, and for cultivating the lighter accomplishments that tend to complete their education as accomplished gentlemen.

568. During this season, the place is thronged by visitors from all parts of the United States. Many of their friends visit them; they are permitted to have social parties, which the visitors are fond of attending, provided with music and attended with dancing. They have the benefit of a dancing-master during this period; and, in connection with the superior society that is convened there at this time, the cadet has the opportunity of learning correct manners, ease of deportment, and a knowledge of the great world, from which he is in the main excluded during the remainder of the year. It is only necessary to caution the cadet not to become too much devoted to this part of his experience, so as to detract from the more serious duties on which, after all, his best energies must be expended to insure success.

NOTE.—During the rebellion, the vacancies from the seceded States have been filled by appointments from the armies occupying those States. Candidates of the proper age are summoned before a board under the direction of the commanding officer, and the appointments are made on the recommendation of the board, after a thorough examination.

PROMOTION.

569. The Act of August 3, 1854, sec. 5, provides that non-commissioned officers who pass an examination of a board of officers under the direction of

the War Department may be promoted to the rank of brevet second lieutenant.

The following is the Regulation with regard to the board:—

"77. A board, to consist of the Professors of Mathematics and Ethics and the Commandant of Cadets, will convene at the Military Academy, on the first Monday of September in every year, for the examination of such non-commissioned officers, for promotion as have already passed the regimental examination prescribed in General Orders No. 17, of October 4, 1854."

570. The following is the Order No. 17 referred to: it will be observed that the above Regulation modifies the first paragraph of the order, with reference to the Board of Examination:—

"GENERAL ORDERS, No. 17.

"WAR DEPARTMENT, ADJUTANT-GENERAL'S OFFICE,
WASHINGTON, October 4, 1854.

"The following regulations have been established to carry out the provisions of the fifth section of the Act of August 4, 1854, relative to the promotion of non-commissioned officers:—

"1. An Army Board, composed of four officers of rank, will be convened, annually, on the first Monday in September, in the city of Washington, for the examination of such non-commissioned officers as may be ordered to appear before them by the War Department.

"2. To aid the Department in the selection of proper candidates for promotion, company commanders will report to their colonels all such non-commissioned officers as, in their opinion, by education, conduct, and services, seem to merit advancement. In these reports must be set forth a description of the candidate, his length of service as non-commissioned officer and as private soldier, his character as to fidelity and sobriety, his physical qualifications and mental abilities, the extent to which his talents have been cultivated, and his fitness generally to discharge the duties of a commissioned officer. If recommended on account of meritorious services, the particular services referred to must be stated in detail. On receiving the reports of company commanders, the colonel will assemble a Board, to consist of four officers of his regiment, of as high rank as the convenience of the service will admit, to make a preliminary examination into the claims and qualifications of those non-commissioned officers who may appear to him deserving promotion. Where the Colonel has not authority to convene such Board, the regimental officers necessary to form it will, on application to the proper department commander, be placed subject to his orders. The Board, constituted as above, will submit a full statement in the case of each candidate examined; and on these statements the colonel will endorse his remarks and forward them, through the head-quarters of the army, to the Adjutant-General, to be laid before the Secretary of War.

"3. The foregoing reports must be transmitted in time to reach Washington by the 1st day of May in each year, and such non-commissioned officers as the Secretary of War may consider suitable candidates for promotion will receive orders from the Adjutant-General's Office to present themselves for examination by the Board to be convened on the first Monday in September following. As a general rule, one-fourth of the vacancies occurring annually in the Army will be filled from the non-commissioned grades. The persons thus appointed shall, as far as practicable, be attached to the regiments in which their meritorious services had been rendered, and will thereafter succeed to vacancies in their particular arm of service according to seniority.

"4. No candidate will be examined who is married; who is under twenty or over twenty-eight years of age; who, in the judgment of the Board, has not the physical ability to endure the exposures of service; who has any deformity of body, or whose moral habits are bad.

"5. The Board, being satisfied of these preliminary points, will proceed to examine each candidate separately—

"*First.* In his knowledge of English Grammar, and ability to read and write with facility and correctness.

"*Second.* In his knowledge of Arithmetic, and his ability in the application of its rules to all practical questions, and in his knowledge of plane and solid Geometry.

"*Third.* In his knowledge of Geography, particularly in reference to the northern continent of America, and in his ability to solve the usual problems on the terrestrial globe. Also in his knowledge of what is usually denominated popular Astronomy.

"*Fourth.* In his knowledge of History, particularly in reference to his own country.

"*Fifth.* In his knowledge of the Constitution of the United States, and of the organization of the Government under it, and of the general principles which regulate international intercourse.

"6. After having completed the examination of all candidates who have presented themselves, the Board will then submit their names to the War Department in order of relative merit. In determining this order, the Board will consider eight as the maximum of the first, fourth, and fifth heads, and ten as the maximum of the second and third heads; and no candidate will be passed by the Board who shall not have received at least half of the number of maximum marks on each head or subject of examination. And any candidate having passed, who is also a graduate from any college, shall be allowed five additional marks in his favor, which shall be taken into the account of his general merit.

"7. In order to give effect, as early as practicable, to the intention of the law, the first general examination of non-commissioned officers, except such as are serving in the Department of New Mexico, will take place at Washington on the second Monday of January next. Those serving in New Mexico will be examined the first Monday in June following. Colonels will accordingly take immediate measures for forwarding, in due season, the reports necessary to aid in the selection of proper candidates to be brought before these first two Boards of Examination.

"By Order of the Secretary of War:

"S. COOPER, *Adjutant-General.*"

571. It is, perhaps, the surest means for a competent man to enter the army as an officer to enlist as a soldier and by attention to his duties be made a non-commissioned officer, and finally appear before the Board for examination. It is a severe school, but sure to succeed if pursued with proper energy and perseverance.

572. During the early part of the rebellion the examinations fell into disuse, and a great many non-commissioned officers were promoted, on account of their gallantry and faithful service, who perhaps would not have passed the board. The

Board of Examination has, however, recently been revived, and the necessity of the case will undoubtedly cause the organization of boards of examination for promotion to the higher grades also, in the course of time.

573. The rule of promotion by seniority has been detrimental in affording no encouragement to the ambitions to improve themselves in the study of their profession; whilst the certainty of a regular advancement encourages the ignorant and idle to content themselves with barely performing their duty, and neglecting all opportunities to improve themselves.

574. It is a great mistake to suppose that when the commission has been obtained there is nothing more to be done, except to draw the pay and display the uniform. In reality, the field of study has just opened, and the most competent, efficient officer finds it necessary to devote a portion of his time to improvement, even if it extend no further than simply to keep himself posted in the changes daily promulgated, in orders, of the laws, regulations, orders, instructions, and rules for the government of the army or its different divisions and detachments.

575. The studies for the military profession cannot be exhausted; and although the officer may succeed to the various grades by virtue of his seniority, it does not follow that he will, therefore, fill them well, or that his ignorance and inefficiency

are not known and condemned. On the contrary, his industry and zeal, whilst it may not bring him rank, will certainly bring him reputation and the respect of his brother officers; and although he may wear the shoulder-strap of a subaltern, he may still be enjoying a reputation and renown which many a general might well envy. A high standing among his fellow-officers in the army is of more value to an officer of proper feeling than all the rank and notoriety that a newspaper reputation or political favor can lavish upon him.

576. An officer of the army should always be a gentleman, sufficiently well educated to appear well in any society, and fully conversant with the duties of his grade in the arm of service to which he belongs. Whatever additional qualifications he possesses will be so much more to aid him in attaining a higher grade, and, although they may not be strictly military they will be an additional ornament to his position, for which he will surely be appreciated and which will always be considered in canvassing his merits to perform the duties to which he will from time to time be assigned.

577. When non-commissioned officers are promoted, they must be discharged; the discharge and final statements to be made out up to the date of acceptance of the commission. Volunteers must be mustered out of the old grade and mustered in in the new. The muster-out and muster-in rolls can be dated back to the time when the officer can furnish

the necessary evidence of having entered upon the duties of his commission, and that he could not be mustered before; otherwise the muster must be dated at the time it is made. The muster, however, cannot in any case be dated prior to the date of commission, nor prior to any muster in which the officer has been mustered in another grade: this would seem to restrict the dating back of the muster to two months at farthest. It sometimes happens that an officer receives his commission where he cannot be mustered for some months; and, as it is prohibited to take him up on the rolls in any capacity until he has been regularly mustered out of the old and mustered in the new grade, the dating back the commission, it seems, cannot be extended beyond the last muster. (See G. O. No. 48, 1863.)

578. When an officer receives a commission, the facilities to be mustered in should, therefore, be at once extended to him by the commanding officers, by either sending or permitting him to go where he can be mustered into service.

579. The introduction of colored troops into our army affords most favorable opportunities for promotion. Any one who is competent may present himself before the board of examiners; and, if he passes the examination, he will be commissioned an officer in a grade proportionate to his qualifications.

580. This arm of the service seems likely to be-

come very popular. The system of examinations which is pursued for obtaining officers is calculated to insure success, as the colored regiments must necessarily be well officered, and good officers will make good troops even out of negroes.

581. Applicants who are in the military service and desiring to be commissioned to command in the colored regiments must obtain recommendations from their commanding officers, and forward them to the Adjutant-General, who will give the necessary authority to appear before the examining board. Civilians must present satisfactory testimonials in order to obtain authority from the Adjutant-General to present themselves, showing that they are of good moral character and standing in the community where they reside.

VETERAN RESERVE CORPS.

582. ALL soldiers who have been incapacitated for active duty, but who are nevertheless able to do garrison duty, may be enlisted or transferred into the Veteran Reserve Corps, with the same pay and allowances as infantry.

This corps is a volunteer organization. The troops composing it are required to serve for the unexpired portion of their term, and re-enlistments are for three years. The organization of the corps is provided for in G.O. Nos. 105, 130, and 173, 1863.

The name of the corps has been changed from Invalid Corps to Veteran Reserve Corps. (General Orders No. 111, 1864.)

583. These orders provide that the officers and men composing the Veteran Reserve Corps shall consist of men of good character, whose disability has occurred in the discharge of their duty, and whose services have been faithful and meritorious.

584. Regimental commanders are required from time to time to make out the lists of officers and men physically disqualified for active field duty, and forward them, through the intermediate commanders, to the Provost-Marshal General at Washington, with the history and merits of each case stated in the column of remarks by all officers through whose hands the lists are required to pass, and who have any knowledge of the cases. (G.O. No. 105, 1863.)

585. When these lists reach the corps or department commander, he issues the order for the transfer of the invalid detachment to the reserve corps, and for it to proceed to the depot for invalids for his army corps or department, which depot is directed in General Orders from the War Department. The detachment must be accompanied by the descriptive lists and clothing accounts of the men. (G.O. No. 173, 1863.)

586. Soldiers who have been honorably discharged on account of disability incurred in the service, and who deem themselves fit for garrison

or other light duty, may re-enlist for three year for service in this corps, provided that they are unfit for service in the field, but fit for garrison duty, that they are deserving, and have been honorably discharged. Men desiring to re-enlist under the foregoing circumstances must present themselves before the Board of Enrolment for the district in which they reside, and be examined by the surgeon of the board, and establish the required facts in each case, to the satisfaction of the board: they can then be enlisted under the regulations prescribed by the Provost-Marshal General.

587. Soldiers receive no increased pay for reenlistment in the Veteran Reserve Corps, nor can they claim any pension, bounty, or increased pay for enlistment or re-enlistment; but no previous claim for pension or bounty will be invalidated by their enlistment in this corps; they can receive only the pay and allowances of United States infantry, and nothing additional.

588. The corps is organized into companies and regiments, and is used for garrisoning forts, towns, and other duties which these troops are capable of performing, and for which able-bodied men would otherwise be required.

589. The invalids of the regular army are organized into companies, and stationed at the recruiting depots of their respective regiments, where they constitute the permanent garrisons. They are not dropped from the rolls of their respective

companies. Should they become fit for field service at any time, they are again returned to their companies. Enlistments for these companies are not allowed; but invalid soldiers, when discharged, may re-enlist in the Volunteer Invalid Corps. As soldiers in the regular army become unfit for field-duty, they are examined by the surgeons and sent to the depots, there to be attached to the invalid companies of their respective regiments. (G.O. No. 290, 1863.)

VETERANS.

590. VOLUNTEERS who have served at least nine months, and who re-enlist, are entitled to be called "*Veteran Volunteers*," and may wear the service chevron showing that they have served one enlistment. (G.O. No. 191, 1863.)

591. Veterans are entitled to one month's advance pay, a premium of two dollars, and bounty amounting in all to four hundred and two dollars, to be paid by instalments as provided in G.O. No. 191, Par. 30. If discharged before the expiration of their enlistment, veterans will receive the balance on the foregoing bounty. The heirs of veterans who die in service will be entitled to the balance of the above bounty remaining unpaid at the time of death.

592. Soldiers who re-enlisted prior to June 25, 1863, and who have complied with the conditions

promulgated in G.O. No. 191 of that date, are entitled to the bounty therein provided; that is, they must have served one enlistment of at least nine months, and been regularly and properly mustered into service. (G.O. No. 216, 1863.)

593. A veteran regiment, to entitle it to be called such, must be composed of at least one-half of its number of men who have served one enlistment of not less than nine months. (G.O. No. 216, 1863.)

594. Recruits—that is, men who have served less than nine months, or who have not seen service at all—who enlisted in old regiments whose terms expire in 1864 and 1865, are entitled to one month's pay, a premium of two dollars, and bounty amounting in all to three hundred and fifteen dollars, to be paid as follows:—

On being mustered into service, and before leaving depot or recruiting station,—

One month's advance pay	$13 00
First instalment of bounty	60 00
Premium	2 00
Total	$75 00
At the first regular pay-day, or two months after muster-in	40 00
At the first regular pay-day after six months' service	40 00
At the first regular pay-day after the end of the first year	40 00
At the first regular pay-day after eighteen months	40 00
At the first regular pay-day after two years	40 00

At the expiration of three years' service, or before,
if discharged, the remainder 40 00
                                                    _____
    Total.............................. $315 00

595. If the Government shall not require these
troops for the full period of their enlistment, and
they be honorably mustered out of service before,
they shall receive, on being mustered out, the
whole amount of bounty remaining unpaid, the
same as if they had served their full term. The foregoing bounty applies to all recruits, both regulars
and volunteers (G. O. No. 338, 1864, and Circular
98, Provost-Marshal General's Office, Nov. 3, 1863).

COLORED TROOPS.

596. The Act of July 17, 1862, section 12, authorizes the President to receive into the service of the
United States persons of African descent, for any
military or naval service for which they may be
found competent. Section 13 of the same Act gives
freedom to the slaves of rebels who enter the service of the United States, and also to the mothers,
wives, and children of such slaves as enter the
service, provided they are the slaves of rebels.

597. On this authority is based the organization
of the colored regiments. The officers appointed by
the President are white men, and selected by a
board of examiners, as stated in par. 579. The

non-commissioned officers may be either white or colored.

598. Colored soldiers receive the same pay, allowances, and bounties and are in all respects on the same footing as white troops. The administration of colored troops is, therefore, the same as that of white troops.

PUNISHMENTS.

599. THE punishment of soldiers for military offences is a subject of much importance not well understood by them, nor is it very clearly defined except in specific cases. This imperfect knowledge on the part of soldiers, and want of a clearly defined system regulating the punishments inflicted for the lighter offences, are the causes of a large number of offences that would not otherwise occur, and of errors on the part of officers, against which the soldiers may justly complain, if they only knew how to do so.

600. The authority to punish is derived from two sources. That obtained from the Articles of War and other statutes is comparatively clear and specific; but that based upon custom is not so well defined. Where the latter commences, and what is the limit to which it may be carried, seems almost entirely dependent on the discrimination of each individual officer.

601. The Articles of War provide for the punishment of all offences therein indicated by sentence of courts-martial. All cases that cannot clearly be placed under a particular article are provided for in the 99th Article. The customary charge in these doubtful cases is "conduct prejudicial to good order and military discipline." The sentence is governed by the "customs of war in like cases."

602. The confinement of soldiers and arrest of non-commissioned officers, and the lighter corporeal punishments, although not authorized by law, are sanctioned by custom; and custom is the common law of the army. The summary punishments sometimes inflicted on soldiers, such as tying them up by the hands, compelling them to carry a loaded knapsack, and similar inflictions, are resorted to in cases of insubordination, unruly conduct, &c., where the usual trial by court-martial or field-officers' court cannot be conveniently had, or when the punishment is likely to be slow and tardy.

603. Soldiers should bear in mind, when they feel aggrieved at the summary punishment inflicted by an officer, that it might have been much worse had he pursued the course indicated by the law or the Articles of War, and that the officer, in inflicting a speedy punishment has only consulted the best interests of the soldier, so far as the necessity of sustaining the discipline of the service will permit.

604. The officer is able to see beforehand that if he prefers charges against the man, an indefinite

period must elapse before a court-martial can be assembled; the soldier must remain in confinement in the mean while: this, added to the sentence which the court would probably inflict, would in reality be a much greater punishment than the officer would himself be likely to inflict on his own responsibility.

605. Extreme cases sometimes occur where an officer exceeds his authority, prompted by personal feeling against the soldier. Such instances, fortunately, are rare; but, as they may occur, a remedy is provided in the following Article of War:—

"ART. 35. If any inferior officer or soldier shall think himself wronged by his captain or other officer, he is to complain thereof to the commanding officer of the regiment, who is hereby required to summon a regimental court-martial, for the doing justice to the complainant; from which regimental court-martial either party may, if he thinks himself still aggrieved, appeal to a general court-martial. But if upon a second hearing, the appeal shall appear vexatious and groundless, the person so appealing shall be punished at the discretion of the said court-martial."

606. When a soldier considers himself wronged, his proper course is to write a statement of his complaint in the following form, which will serve as a form for communications on any other subject when a soldier may desire to correspond with an officer.—

CAMP CHASE, OHIO, January 21, 1864.

Sir:—

I have the honor to call the attention of the commanding officer of the regiment to certain acts of ill treatment

that I have received at the hands of Lieut. J—— C——, 2d
Lieut. 1st U. S. Infantry. (Here give the circumstances of
the ill treatment in detail.)

Respectfully submitted for the action of the commanding officer of the regiment.

Very respectfully, your ob't serv't,

C—— D——,

Private Co. A, 1st U.S. Infantry.

Lieut. L—— M——,

  lst Lieutenant and Adjutant,

    1st U. S. Infantry.

        Approved and forwarded,

          A—— B——,

            Capt. Company A, 1st U. S. Infantry.

607. This communication is addressed to the adjutant of the regiment, but is first submitted to the
commanding officer of the company, who will endorse his views upon it before sending it up to the
adjutant.

608. Such a communication should not be sent,
however, without good cause, as it is liable to react
on the soldier; for, if soldiers should send up such
communications for every trivial matter in which
they consider themselves aggrieved, it is easy to
see to what extent it might be carried. In their subordinate positions, they are liable to entertain many
ill-founded ideas.

609. Private soldiers, when charged with any offence, are confined under guard until their cases
are acted on. In the mean time, it is the custom that
prisoners confined under guard be kept employed

at such work as the commanding office may direct,—usually clearing the grounds about the camp or garrison, cutting wood, &c. Prisoners, unless employed, would soon become sick.

THE COURT-MARTIAL.

610. WHEN enlisted men find themselves arraigned before a court-martial, a knowledge of how they should conduct themselves on trial is essential.

611. The charges are usually made known to the prisoner before trial. In fact, he is entitled to a copy of the charges against him beforehand and should make up his mind as to what will be his defense. He may be permitted to have counsel in the court, if he requests it.

612. When the court is ready to proceed with the trial, the prisoner is brought in. The names of the members are called over by the recorder or judge-advocate; the order convening the court is then read over, and the prisoner then asks permission to introduce his counsel into the court-room. He then is asked if he has any objections to be tried by any member on the court. If he has any objection, he must state it: the objection may be either against the right of the court to try him, or to the relevancy of the charges, or to some members of the court. The court deliberates on the

objections, and he is informed of the result, whether his objections are sustained or not.

613. The court is next sworn in the presence of the prisoner, and the room is then cleared of the witnesses, and the charges are read to the prisoner, and he is asked how he pleads, first to the specifications, and then to the charge, "Guilty, or not guilty." If the prisoner does not answer, he is regarded as having plead "not guilty."

614. The witnesses that give evidence against the prisoner are called first. They are sworn by the recorder or judge-advocate, and first examined by him, then by the prisoner, and finally by the court. The prisoner writes out or dictates his questions to the recorder, who writes them down, and also the answers. The witnesses called by the prisoner are first questioned by him, then by the recorder, and then by the court.

615. When all the witnesses are examined, the prisoner makes his defense, if he has any to make, and a reasonable length of time will be allowed him if he wishes to write it, or the recorder will take it down if he delivers it verbally; or this may be done by the counsel for the prisoner. The recorder or judge-advocate can reply if he chooses. If the prisoner has no prospect of disproving the charges against him, his best course is to plead guilty, and rely upon his statement in defence; or he may bring witnesses to prove his previous good character; or he may even introduce testimony

mitigating the circumstances of his guilt, and to the mercy of the court.

616. During the trial it is customary to remove the shackles or handcuffs from the prisoner. After the trial, the prisoner is sent back to await the publication of the proceedings, which requires time. They are first sent to the officer ordering the court; and, if the sentence involves death, it requires the approval of the President, except in time of war, in the field, in the case of a spy or deserter, or of mutiny or murder, when it may be acted on by the commander of the army in the field. If the officer ordering the court is subordinate to the commander of the army, he may endorse final action on the proceedings, unless they extend to imprisonment in a penitentiary, or loss of life of the enlisted man, when they must be sent to the commander of the army. If the commander is himself the officer that ordered the court, then he must send the proceedings up to the President; if the soldier is sentenced to the penitentiary or death, unless in the case of a spy or deserter, or of mutiny or murder, in these cases he may act finally himself.

617. The legal punishments of soldiers are specified in the following Regulations, viz.:

"895. The legal punishments for soldiers by sentence of a court-martial according to the offence, and the jurisdiction of the court, are—death; confinement; confinement on bread-and-water-diet; solitary confinement;

hard labor; ball and chain; forfeiture of pay and allowances; discharges from service; and reprimands, and, when non-commissioned officers, reduction to the ranks. Ordnance sergeants and hospital stewards, however, though liable to discharge, may not be reduced. Nor are they to be tried by regimental or garrison courts-martial, unless by special permission of the department commander. Solitary confinement, or confinement on bread and water, shall not exceed fourteen days at a time, with intervals between the periods of such confinement not less than such periods; and not exceeding eighty-four days in any one year."

618. General courts-martial are not limited in the penalties they may inflict. Regimental and garrison courts-martial are limited in their powers by the following Article of War, viz.:—

"Art. 67. No garrison or regimental court-martial shall have the power to try capital cases or commissioned officers; neither shall they inflict a fine exceeding one month's pay, nor imprison, nor put to hard labor, any non-commissioned officer or soldier for a longer time than one month."

619. By sec. 7 of the Act of July 17, 1862, a field officer is authorized to act in all cases where a regimental or garrison court would have jurisdiction. The field officer tries the case instead of the court, and the proceedings should be similar, as far as possible, to those of a regimental or garrison court.

620. A soldier, seeking to have his sentence remitted by reason of subsequent good conduct, or in consequence of the development of new or addi-

tional testimony in his favor, may do so by submitting the facts in the case to the officer who ordered the court and revised the proceedings, or to his successor.

621. Sec. 29, Act of March 3, 1863, contains a proviso, "that if the prisoner be in close confinement, the trial shall not be delayed for a period longer than sixty days." Therefore, at the expiration of sixty days, the prisoner can lawfully claim to be tried, or released from close confinement until he can be tried.

622. When prisoners are in confinement waiting to be tried by civil authority, they cannot claim payment for any portion of the time they are so confined, unless discharged without trial, or by trial and acquitted; and company commanders are required to state on their rolls the period of such confinement, and how discharged. (Circular 21, War Department, Adjutant-General's Office, March 1, 1864.) Soldiers convicted by civil authority are dishonorably discharged the service.

623. Soldiers should know that for all offences against persons or property, and for all crimes, they are as amenable to the civil authority as civilians, and can he arrested and tried the same as any other person.

PRISONERS OF WAR.

624. WHEN soldiers are captured by the enemy, they must expect to be closely guarded and subject to great inconvenience. The customs of war, however, entitle the prisoner to certain privileges. He should be permitted to keep all his personal effects that can readily be transported with him and that cannot be used to effect his escape. If his money is taken from him, it should be used to supply his wants, and the balance returned when he is released or exchanged; he is entitled to food and clothing; he is entitled to kind and considerate treatment as long as he is submissive and obedient, and can claim to be treated as an ordinary prisoner of war. Guerrillas, spies, &c. are not ordinary prisoners of war, and are, therefore, at the mercy of their captors.

625. "A prisoner of war is a public enemy, armed or attached to the hostile army for active aid, who has fallen into the hands of the captor, either fighting or wounded, on the field or in the hospital, by individual surrender or by capitulation." (G.O. No. 100, 1863, Par. 49.)

626. A prisoner of war, in order to claim the immunities of such a situation, must belong to the hostile army in some authorized way, or be in the employ of the Government in some official capacity, and as an enemy he must first throw down his

arms, and ask for quarter, and be submissive to his captors.

627. Troops using the enemy's uniform or flag to deceive, are at the mercy of their captors when taken. If captured clothing is used, it should be worn with some distinctive mark or badge indicative of their character.

628. Prisoners who have escaped and are recaptured should not be punished for escaping, although they may be subjected to stricter confinement. It is the duty of prisoners to escape if they can. They should, therefore, avoid any parole which would prevent them from taking advantage of any opportunities to escape.

629. Enlisted men are prohibited from taking a parole, except through an officer. A soldier giving his parole without the approval thereto of his commanding officer, subjects himself to the penalty of desertion, and the parole is void. It is only admissible for a soldier to parole himself when he has suffered long imprisonment and been properly separated from his command, without the possibility of being paroled through an officer. (G. O. No. 49, 1863.)

630. Paroling on the battle-field is prohibited; and no parole should be taken or given under any circumstances until the prisoners are secured beyond the possibility of recapture. When paroles are given, it is done "by the exchange of signed duplicates of a written document, in which the

same and rank of the parties paroled are correctly stated."

631. Paroles are of two kinds,—a *military parole* and a *parole of honor*. A military parole is where the prisoner is released from custody, and pledges himself not to take up arms against his captors until properly exchanged. A parole of honor is where the prisoner, still under the control of his captors, pledges himself to do or not to do a certain thing, so far as he himself is concerned; as where for the privilege of being released from prison he promises to make no attempt to escape. (G. O. No. 207, 1863.)

632. Neither parole should be given except under circumstances that would manifestly justify their being given. The prisoner is performing a service to his own cause in compelling his captors to guard and provide for him, and his own Government is supposed to take all the necessary measures for procuring his proper exchange.

633. The inhabitants of a hostile country are not treated as foes so long as they remain peaceable and submissive to the forces occupying. Individuals are to be treated as spies and guerrillas who perform any overt acts of hostility or give information to the enemy. The inhabitants of the country are treated as prisoners of war only when they rise *en masse* to repel the invading forces.

634. Prisoners of war are entitled to pay during

their imprisonment the same as if they were off duty. (G.O. No. 9, 1862.)

"The following plan for paying to the families of officers and soldiers in the service of the United States, who are or may become prisoners of war, sums due them by the Government, having been approved by the President, it is published for the information of all concerned.

"Payment will be made to persons presenting a written authority from a prisoner to draw his pay; or, without such authority, to his wife, the guardian of his minor children, or his widowed mother, in the order named.

"Application for such pay must be made to the senior paymaster of the district, in which the regiment of the prisoner is serving, and must be accompanied by the certificate of a Judge of a Court of the United States, of a District Attorney of the United States, or of some other party under the seal of a court of record of the State in which the applicant is a resident, setting forth that the said applicant is the wife of the prisoner, the guardian of his children, or his widowed mother, and, if occupying either of the last two relationships towards him, that there is no one in existence who is more nearly related, according to the above classification.

"Payments will be made to parties thus authorized and identified, on their receipts made out in the manner that would be required of the prisoner himself, at least one month's pay being in all cases retained by the United States. The officer making the payment will see that it is entered on the last previous muster-roll for the payment of the prisoner's company, or will report, if those rolls are not in his possession, to the senior paymaster of the district, who will either attend to the entry or give notice of the payment to the Paymaster-General, if the rolls have been forwarded to his office." (G.O. No. 90, 1861.)

635. Prisoners of war are also entitled to pay for rations during the period of their imprisonment, which will be commuted to them by the Subsistence Department at the cost price of the ration. (G.O. No. 24, 1862.)

DESERTERS.

636. DESERTION is one of the most serious military crimes that a soldier can commit, and is punishable with death in time of war, and is the only offence for which flogging is now allowed, in time of peace, in the army. Nor can a soldier ever free himself from the penalties of desertion except by surrendering himself for trial or trusting to pardon. He is constantly liable to be apprehended by any one who may be tempted by the reward offered; and the constant fear which a deserter must experience should deter the soldier from the act, and make him bear with the hardships to which he may be temporarily exposed.

637. Desertion consists in leaving the command with the intention of not returning to it, after having been duly enlisted or mustered into service. It is only necessary that the soldier shall have received pay in some form to make him guilty of the

crime of desertion (Art. 20) before enlistment, if he leaves the service without proper authority.

638. The reward now offered for deserters is thirty dollars. Any one may apprehend a deserter and claim the reward. The expenses of his apprehension are charged against him, and he is required to make good the time lost by his desertion, even when he is restored to duty without trial. The officer who has authority to order a court-martial to try a deserter is competent to restore him to duty without trial; and it is sometimes done with the conditions that he forfeit all pay and allowances due him up to the date of his surrender or apprehension, and that he make good his time lost, and pay the expenses of his apprehension.

639. A soldier cannot absent himself from his company or command without exposing himself to the penalties of desertion, without some authority in writing, as an *order*, *furlough*, *pass*, *permit*, or something to show that he is on duty or has permission.

640. A soldier wishing to be absent, if for two or three days or a certain number of hours, should provide himself with a *pass* or *permit* in the following form, which is written out and presented for signature to the officers indicated, and in the order of signature:—

FORT SCOTT, KANSAS, Jan. 1, 1862.

Private John Smith, Company "A," 1st U. S. Infantry, has permission to be absent for the purpose of (here state the object of the absence) until Retreat.

JOHN BROWN,
1st Sergt. Co. "A," 1st U. S. Inft'y.

A— B—,
Capt. Co. "A," 1st U. S. Inft'y.

Approved, J— D—,
Col. 1st U. S. Inft'y, Com'dg.

641. Sometimes the orders may require the pass to be signed by the brigade or division commander, or even still higher authority. Orders are usually issued in each army regulating the matter of passes and furloughs, and are changed from time to time, according to circumstances.

642. For longer periods, furloughs are given according to a form, page 34, Revised Regulations. Blanks for furloughs are usually to be had at regimental or post head-quarters.

643. Soldiers should bear in mind that unless they return punctually at the expiration of their pass or furlough, they are liable to be treated as deserters. Soldiers are entitled to commutation for their rations whilst absent on furlough, if not drawn in kind from the commissary.

OBEDIENCE TO ORDERS.

644. OBEDIENCE to the orders of their superiors is enjoined upon officers and enlisted men, and the instances are extremely rare where an inferior can assume the responsibility of disobeying the orders of his superior. The illegality of the orders may sometimes be so apparent that an inferior can assume the responsibility of disobeying them; but, as a rule, such a course would involve him in greater difficulties than to obey them.

645. Generally, however, soldiers are liable to act upon some erroneous impression that they are required to do more than their proper share of duty, and that, therefore, the officer has no right to require such duty from them. In such cases, the proper course for the soldier is to obey the order, and complain of the injustice of the treatment afterward. It must be an order manifestly illegal that can justify positive disobedience.

646. Disobedience of orders is a serious offence, and is even punishable with death. (Art. 9.) It must, however, be a lawful order; but the party required to execute the order is the last person entitled to decide upon its legality. It is probable that the person ordering is the most competent to decide this point. There are many orders which may be improper on the part of the superior that the inferior could not therefore assume the responsibility of

disobeying. As a rule, in such cases, the responsibility rests with the officer giving the order.

647. An order, when it is legal, is binding upon the person to whom it is given, whether made by a corporal or a general. The latter has more power to enforce his order than the former, but obedience is due as much to one as to the other.

648. In the execution of orders, much depends upon a correct understanding of them, as also upon giving them in a clear and decisive manner. A good officer, having a perfect understanding of what he wishes done, will give his orders in a clear and distinct manner, and will take pains to see that they are understood; whilst, on the other hand, a good soldier will not start to execute an order until he understands fully what he has got to do, and then, if conscientious, will execute it to the best of his ability.

649. Important orders should always be written; and non-commissioned officers and soldiers are recommended to carry a memorandum-book and pencil, and always write down their orders and instructions: It serves the memory, and the order is obtained correct.

ARTICLES OF WAR.

650. SOLDIERS should know that the Articles of War are a code of laws passed by Congress for the

government of the army. The most of them pre-scribe penalties for certain crimes and offences. The Articles of War were nearly all passed at one time, but many laws have been made since, from time to time, that are of the same nature, and have all the force of the Articles of War.

651. Article 101 prescribes that the Articles of War shall be read and published once in every six months to every garrison, regiment, troop, or com-pany mustered, or to be mustered, into the service of the United States. This article is rarely complied with, but no one can claim immunity from them be-cause they have not been published as required. The Regulations for the Army are often confounded with the Articles of War; but they do not have the same force, and are liable to be changed at any time by the Secretary of War in general orders.

652. The following are all the Articles affecting soldiers; and they should be carefully read and studied by every enlisted man in the service. With the exception of 10, 20, and 87, they remain un-changed. The changes are indicated by the notes appended.

"ART. 2. It is earnestly recommended to all officers and soldiers diligently to attend divine service; and all officers who shall behave indecently or irreverently at any place of divine worship shall, if commissioned officers, be brought before a general court-martial, there to be pub-licly and severely reprimanded by the President; if non-commissioned officers or soldiers, every person so offending shall, for his first offence, forfeit one-sixth of a dollar, to be deducted out of his next pay; for the second offence, he shall not only forfeit a like sum, but be confined twenty-four hours; and for every like offence, shall suffer and pay in like manner; which money, so forfeited, shall be applied, by the captain or senior officer of the troop or company, to the use of the sick soldiers of the company or troop to which the offender belongs.

"ART. 3. Any non-commissioned officer or soldier who shall use any profane oath or execration, shall incur the penalties expressed in the foregoing article; and a commissioned officer shall forfeit and pay, for each and every such offense, one dollar, to be applied as in the preceding article.

"ART. 5. Any officer or soldier who shall use contemptuous or disrespectful words against the President of the United States, against the Vice-President thereof, against the Congress of the United States, or against the Chief Magistrate or Legislature of any of the United States, in which he may be quartered, if a commissioned officer, shall be cashiered, or otherwise punished, as a court-martial shall direct; if a non-commissioned officer or soldier, he shall suffer such punishment as shall be inflicted on him by the sentence of a court-martial.

"ART. 6. Any officer or soldier who shall behave himself with contempt or disrespect toward his commanding officer, shall be punished, according to the nature of his offence, by the judgment of a court-martial.

"ART. 7. Any officer or soldier who shall begin, excite, cause, or join in, any mutiny or sedition, in any troop or company in the service of the United States, or in any party, post, detachment, or guard, shall suffer death, or such other punishment as by a court-martial shall be inflicted.

"ART. 8. Any officer, non-commissioned officer, or soldier, who being present at any mutiny or sedition, does not use his utmost endeavor to suppress the same, or, coming to the knowledge of any intended mutiny does not, without delay, give information thereof to his commanding officer, shall be punished by the sentence of a court-martial with death, or otherwise, according to the nature of his offence.

"ART. 9. Any officer or soldier who shall strike his superior officer, or draw or lift up any weapon, or offer any violence against him, being in the execution of his office, on any pretence whatsoever, or shall disobey any lawful command of his superior officer, shall suffer death, or such other punishment as shall, according to the nature of his offence, be inflicted upon him by the sentence of a court-martial.

"ART. 10. Every non-commissioned officer or soldier, who shall enlist himself in the service of the United States, shall, at the time of his so enlisting, or within six days afterward, have the Articles for the government of the armies of the United States read to him, and shall, by the officer who enlisted him, or by the commanding officer of the troop or company into which he was enlisted, be taken before the next justice of the peace, or chief magistrate of any city or town corporate, not being an officer of the army,* or where recourse cannot be had to the civil magistrate, before the judge advocate, and in his presence shall take the following oath or affirmation: 'I, A. B., do solemnly swear, or affirm (as the case may be), that I will bear true allegiance to the United States of America, and that I will serve them honestly and faithfully against all their enemies or op-

---

*By Sect. 11 of Chap. 38, August 3, 1861, the oath of enlistment and re-enlistment may be administered by any commissioned officer of the army.

posers whatsoever; and observe and obey the orders of the
President of the United States, and the orders of the officers appointed over me, according to the Rules and Articles
for the government of the armies of the United States.'
Which justice, magistrate, or judge advocate is to give to
the officer a certificate, signifying that the man enlisted did
take the said oath or affirmation.

"ART. 11. After a non-commissioned officer or soldier
shall have been duly enlisted and sworn, he shall not be
dismissed the service without a discharge in writing; and
no discharge granted to him shall be sufficient which is
not signed by a field officer of the regiment to which he
belongs, or commanding officer, where no field officer
of the regiment is present; and no discharge shall be
given to a non-commissioned officer or soldier before his
term of service has expired, but by order of the President, the Secretary of War, the commanding officer of a
department, or the sentence of a general court-martial;
nor shall a commissioned officer be discharged the service but by order of the President of the United States,
or by sentence of a general court-martial.

"ART. 12. Every colonel, or other officer commanding a
regiment, troop, or company, and actually quartered with
it, may give furloughs to non-commissioned officers or soldiers, in such numbers, and for so long a time, as he shall
judge to be most consistent with the good of the service;
and a captain, or other inferior officer, commanding a troop
or company, or in any garrison, fort, or barrack of the
United States (his field officer being absent), may give furloughs to non-commissioned officers or soldiers, for a time
not exceeding twenty days in six months, but not to more
than two persons to be absent at the same time, expect-
ing some extraordinary occasion should require it.

"Art. 20. All officers and soldiers who have received pay, or have been duly enlisted in the service of the United States, and shall be convicted of having deserted the same, shall suffer death, or such other punishment as, by sentence of a court-martial, shall be inflicted.*

"Art. 21. Any non-commissioned officer or soldier who shall, without leave from his commanding officer, absent himself from his troop, company, or detachment, shall upon being convicted thereof, be punished according to the nature of his offence, at the discretion of a court-martial.

"Art. 22. No non-commissioned officer or soldier shall enlist himself in any other regiment, troop, or company, without a regular discharge from the regiment, troop, or company in which he last served, on the penalty of being reputed a deserter, and suffering accordingly. And in case any officer shall knowingly receive and entertain such non-commissioned officer or soldier, or shall not, after his being discovered to be a deserter, immediately confine him, and give notice thereof to the corps in which he last served, the said officer shall, by a court-martial, be cashiered.

"Art. 23. Any officer or soldier who shall be convicted of having advised or persuaded any other officer or soldier to desert the service of the United States, shall suffer death, or such other punishment as shall be inflicted upon him by the sentence of a court-martial.*

"Art. 24. No officer or soldier shall use any reproachful or provoking speeches or gestures to another, upon pain, if an officer, of being put in arrest; if a soldier, confined, and of asking pardon of the party offended in the presence of his commanding officer.

---

*No officer or soldier in the army of the United States shall be subject to the punishment of death, for desertion in time of peace. —*Act 29th. May, 1830.*

"ART. 25. No officer or soldier shall send a challenge to another officer or soldier, to fight a duel, or accept a challenge if sent, upon pain, if a commissioned officer, of being cashiered; if a non-commissioned officer or soldier, if suffering corporal punishment, at the discretion of a court-martial.

"ART. 26. If any commissioned or non-commissioned officer commanding a guard shall knowingly or willingly suffer any person whatsoever to go forth to fight a duel, he shall be punished as a challenger; and all seconds, promoters, and carriers of challenges, in order to duels, shall be deemed principals, and be punished accordingly. And it shall be the duty of every officer commanding an army, regiment, company, post, or detachment, who is knowing to a challenge being given or accepted by any officer, non-commissioned officer, or soldier, under his command, or has reason to believe the same to be the case, immediately to arrest and bring to trial such offenders.

"ART. 27. All officers, of what condition soever, have power to part and quell all quarrels, frays, and disorders, though the persons concerned should belong to another regiment, troop, or company; and either to order officers into arrest, or non-commissioned officers or soldiers into confinement, until their proper superior officers shall be acquainted therewith; and whosoever shall refuse to obey such officer (though of an inferior rank), or shall draw his sword upon him, shall be punished at the discretion of a general court-martial.

"ART. 28. Any officer or soldier who shall upbraid another for refusing a challenge, shall himself be punished as a challenger; and all officers and soldiers are hereby discharged from any disgrace or opinion of disadvantage which might arise from their having refused to accept of challenges, as they will only have acted in obedience to the laws, and done their duty as good soldiers who subject themselves to discipline.

"ART. 29. No sutler shall be permitted to sell any kind of liquors or victuals, or to keep their houses or shops open for the entertainment of soldiers after nine at night, or before the beating of the reveille, or upon Sundays, during divine service or sermon, on the penalty of being dismissed from all future sutling.

"ART. 30. All officers commanding in the field, forts, barracks, or garrisons of the United States, are hereby required to see that the persons permitted to sutler shall supply the soldiers with good and wholesome provisions, or other articles, at a reasonable price, as they shall be answerable for their neglect.

"ART. 32. Every officer commanding in quarters, garrisons, or on the march, shall keep good order, and, to the utmost of his power, redress all abuses or disorders which may be committed by any officer or soldier under his command; if, upon complaint made to him of officers or soldiers beating or otherwise ill-treating any person or disturbing fairs or markets, or committing any kind or riots, to the disquieting of the citizens of the United States, he, the said commander, who shall refuse or omit to see justice done to the offender or offenders, and reparation made to the party or parties injured, as far as part of the offender's pay shall enable him or them, shall, upon proof thereof, be cashiered, or otherwise punished, as a general court-martial shall direct.

"ART. 33. When any commissioned officer or soldier shall be accused of a capital crime, or of having used violence, or committed any offence against the person or property of any citizen of any of the United States, such as is punishable by the known laws of the land, the commanding officer and officers of every regiment, troop, or company, to which the person or persons so accused shall belong, are hereby required, upon application duly made by, or in behalf of, the party or parties injured, to use their utmost endeavors to deliver over such accused person or persons to the civil magistrate, and likewise to be aiding and assisting to the officers of justice in apprehending and securing the person or persons so accused, in order to bring him or them to trial. If any commanding officer or officers shall willfully neglect, or shall refuse, upon the application aforesaid, to deliver over such accused person or persons to the civil magistrates, or to be aiding and assisting to the officers of justice in apprehending such person or persons, the officer or officers so offending shall be cashiered.

"ART. 35. If any inferior officer or soldier shall think himself wronged by his captain or other officer, he is to complain thereto to the commanding officer of the regiment, who is hereby required to summon a regimental court-martial, for the doing justice to the complainant; from which regimental court-martial either party may, if he thinks himself still aggrieved, appeal to a general court-martial. But if, upon a second hearing, the appeal shall appear vexatious andgroundless, the person so appealing shall be punished at the discretion of the said court-martial.

"ART. 37. Any non-commissioned officer or soldier who shall be convicted at a regimental court-martial of having sold, or designedly, or through neglect, wasted the ammunition delivered out to him, to be employed in the service of the United States, shall be punished at the discretion of such court.

"ART. 38. Every non-commissioned officer or soldier who shall be convicted before a court-martial of having sold, lost, or spoiled, through neglect, his horse, arms, clothes, or accoutrements, shall undergo such weekly stoppages (not exceeding the half of his pay) as such court-martial shall judge sufficient, for repairing the loss or damage; and shall suffer confinement, or such other corporeal punishment as his crime shall deserve.

"ART. 39. Every officer who shall be convicted before a court-martial of having embezzled or misapplied any money with which he may have been intrusted, for the payment of the men under his command, or for enlisting men into the service, or for other purposes, if a commissioned officer, shall be cashiered, and compelled to refund the money; if a non-commissioned officer, shall be reduced to the ranks, be put under stoppages until the money be made good, and suffer such corporeal punishment as such court-martial shall direct.

"ART. 40. Every captain of a troop or company is charged with the arms, accoutrements, ammunition, clothing, or other warlike stores belonging to the troop or company under his command, which he is to be accountable for to his colonel in case of their being lost, spoiled, or damaged, not by unavoidable accidents, or on actual service.

"ART. 41. All non-commissioned officers and soldiers who shall be found one mile from the camp without leave, in writing, from their commanding officer, shall suffer such punishment as shall be inflicted upon them by the sentence of a court-martial.

"ART. 42. No officer or soldier shall lie out of his quarters, garrison, or camp, without leave from his superior officer, upon penalty of being punished according to the nature of his offence, by the sentence of a court-martial.

"ART. 43. Every non-commissioned officer and soldier shall retire to his quarters or tent at the beating of the retreat; in default of which he shall be punished according to the nature of his offence.

"ART. 44. No officer, non-commissioned officer, or soldier shall fail in repairing, at the time fixed, to the place of parade, of exercise, or other rendezvous appointed by his commanding officer, if not prevented by sickness or some other evident necessity, or shall go from the said place of rendezvous without leave from his commanding officer, before he shall be regularly dismissed or relieved, on the penalty of being punished, according to the nature of his offence, by the sentence of a court-martial.

"ART. 45. Any commissioned officer who shall be found drunk on his guard, party, or other duty, shall be cashiered. Any non-commissioned officer or soldier so offending shall suffer such corporeal punishment as shall be inflicted by the sentence of a court-martial.

"ART. 46. Any sentinel who shall be found sleeping upon his post, or shall leave it before he shall be regularly relieved, shall suffer death, or such other punishment as shall be inflicted by the sentence of a court-martial.

"ART. 47. No soldier belonging to any regiment, troop, or company shall hire another to do his duty for him, or be excused from duty but in cases of sickness, disability, or leave of absence; and every such soldier found guilty of hiring his duty, as also the party so hired to do another's duty, shall be punished at the discretion of a regimental court-martial.

"ART. 48. And every non-commissioned officer conniving at such hiring of duty aforesaid, shall be reduced; and every commissioned officer knowing and allowing such ill practices in the service, shall be punished by the judgment of a general court-martial.

"ART. 50. Any officer or soldier who shall, without urgent necessity, or without the leave of his superior officer, quit his guard, platoon, or division, shall be punished according to the nature of his offence, by the sentence of a court-martial.

"ART. 51. No officer or soldier shall do violence to any person who brings provisions or other necessaries to the camp, garrison, or quarters of the forces of the United States, employed in any parts out of the said States, upon pain of death, or such other punishment as a court-martial shall direct.

"ART. 52. Any officer or soldier who shall misbehave himself before the enemy, run away, or shamefully abandon any fort, post, or guard which he or they may be commanded to defend, or speak words inducing others to do the like, or shall cast away his arms and ammunition, or who shall quit his post or colors to plunder and pillage every such offender, being duly convicted thereof, shall suffer death, or such other punishment as shall be ordered by the sentence of a general court-martial.

"ART. 53. Any person belonging to the armies of the United States who shall make known the watchword to any person who is not entitled to receive it according to the rules and discipline of war, or shall presume to give a parole or watchword different from what he received shall suffer death, or such other punishment as shall be ordered by the sentence of a general court-martial.

"ART. 54. All officers and soldiers are to behave themselves orderly in quarters and on their march; and whoever shall commit any waste or spoil, either in walks of trees, parks, warrens, fish-ponds, houses, or gardens, cornfields enclosures of meadows, or shall maliciously destroy any property whatsoever belonging to the inhabitants of the United States, unless by order of the then commander-in-chief of the armies of the said States, shall (besides such penalties as they are liable to by law) be punished according to the nature and degree of the offence, by the judgment of a regimental or general court-martial.

"ART. 55. Whosoever, belonging to the armies of the United States in foreign parts, shall force a safeguard, shall suffer death.

"ART. 56. Whosoever shall relieve the enemy with money, victuals, or ammunition, or shall knowingly harbor or protect an enemy, shall suffer death, or such other punishment as shall be ordered by the sentence of a court-martial.

"ART. 57. Whosoever shall be convicted of holding correspondence with, or giving intelligence to, the enemy, either directly or indirectly, shall suffer death, or such other punishment as shall be ordered by the sentence of a court-martial.

"ART. 58. All public stores taken in the enemy's camp, towns, forts, or magazines, whether of artillery, ammunition, clothing, forage, or provisions, shall be secured for the service of the United States; for the neglect of which the commanding officer is to be answerable.

"ART. 59. If any commander of any garrison, fortress, or post shall be compelled, by the officers and soldiers under his command, to give up to the enemy, or to abandon it, the commissioned officers, non-commissioned officers, or soldiers who shall be convicted of having so offended, shall suffer death, or such other punishment as shall be inflicted upon them by the sentence of a court-martial.

"ART. 60. All sutlers and retainers to the camp, and all persons whatsoever, serving with the armies of the United States in the field, though not enlisted soldiers, are to be subject to orders, according to the rules and discipline of war.

"ART. 67. No garrison or regimental court-martial shall have the power to try capital cases or commissioned officers; neither shall they inflict a fine exceeding one month's pay, nor imprison, nor put to hard labor, any non-commissioned officer or soldier for a longer time than one month.

"ART. 70. When a prisoner, arraigned before a general court-martial, shall, from obstinacy and deliberate design, stand mute, or answer foreign to the purpose, the court may proceed to trial and judgment as if the prisoner had regularly pleaded not guilty, "Art. 76. No person whatsoever shall use any menacing words, signs, or gestures, in presence of a court-martial or shall cause any disorder or riot, or disturb their proceedings, on the penalty of being punished at the discretion of the said court-martial

"ART. 78. Non-commissioned officers and soldiers, charged with crimes, shall be confined until tried by court-martial, or released by proper authority.

"ART. 79. No officer or soldier who shall be put in arrest shall continue in confinement more than eight days; or until such time as a court-martial can be assembled.

"ART. 87.* No person shall be sentenced to suffer death but by the concurrence of two-thirds of the members of a general court-martial, nor except in the cases herein expressly mentioned; *nor shall more than fifty lashes be inflicted on any offender at the discretion of a court-martial;* and no officer, non-commissioned officer, sol-

---

*So much of these rules and articles as authorized the infliction of corporeal punishment by stripes or lashes, was specially repealed by Act of 16th May, 1812. By Act of 2d March, 1833, the repealing act was repealed, so far as it applied to the crime of desertion, which, of course, revived the punishment by lashes for that offence. Flogging was totally abolished by Sec. 3 of Chap. 49, August 5, 1861.

dier, or follower of the army, shall be tried a second time for the same offence.

"ART. 88. No person shall be liable to be tried and punished by a general court-martial for any offence which shall appear to have been committed more than two years before the issuing of the order for such trial, unless the person, by reason of having absented himself, or some other manifest impediment, shall not have been amenable to justice within that period.

"ART. 95. When any non-commissioned officer or soldier shall die, or be killed in the service of the United States, the then commanding officer of the troop or company shall, in the presence of two other commissioned officers, take an account of what effects he died possessed of, above his arms and accoutrements, and transmit the same to the Department of War, which said effects are to be accounted for and paid to the representatives of such deceased non-commissioned officer or soldier. And in case any of the officers, so authorized to take care of the effects of deceased officers and soldiers, should, before they have accounted to their representatives for the same, have occasion to leave the regiment or post, by preferment or otherwise, they shall, before they be permitted to quit the same, deposit in the hands of the commanding officer, or of the assistant military agent, all the effects of such deceased non-commissioned officers and soldiers in order that the same may be secured for, and paid to, their respective representatives.

"ART. 97. The officers and soldiers of any troops, whether militia or others, being mustered and in pay of the United States, shall, at all times and in all places, when joined or acting in conjunction with the regular forces of the United States, be governed by these rules and Articles of War, and shall be subject to be tried by courts-martial, in like manner with the officers and soldiers in the regular forces; save only that such courts-martial shall be composed entirely of militia officers.

"ART. 99. All crimes not capital, and all disorders and neglects which officers and soldiers may be guilty of to the prejudice of good order and military discipline, though not mentioned in the foregoing Articles of War, are to be taken cognizance of by a general or regimental court-martial, according to the nature and degree of the offence, and be punished at their discretion.

"ART. 101. The foregoing articles are to be read and published, once in every six months, to every garrison, regiment, troop, or company, mustered, or to be mustered, in the service of the United States, and are to be duly observed and obeyed by all officers and soldiers who are, or shall be, in said service."

[APPROVED, April 10, 1806.]

PRINCIPLES OF FIRING.

653. TARGET practice will enable soldiers to learn the use of their fire-arms, in the course of time; but, if they fully understand the principles of firing, their practice will be materially aided. The following is taken from the "Instructions for Field Artillery," and is as applicable to small arms as to cannon.

"POINTING AND RANGES."

"To point a piece is to place it in such a position that the shot may reach the object it is intended to strike. To

do this, the axis of the trunnions being horizontal, the line of metal, called also the natural line of sight, must be so directed as to pass through the object, and then the elevation given to the piece to throw the shot the required distance. The *direction* is given from the trail, and the elevation from the breech; the trail being traversed by a handspike, and the breech raised or depressed by an elevating screw.

"The *axis of the piece* coincides with that of the cylinder of the bore.

"The *line of sight* in pointing is the line of direction from the eye to the object. It lies in a vertical plane, passing through, or parallel to, the axis of the piece.

"The *angle of sight* is the angle which the line of sight makes with the axis of the piece.

"The *natural line of sight* is the straight line passing through the highest points of the base ring, and the swell of the muzzle, muzzle sight, or muzzle band.

"The *natural angle of sight* is the angle which the natural line of sight makes with the axis of the piece.

"The *dispart of a piece* is half the difference between the diameters of the base ring and swell of the muzzle, or the muzzle band. It is therefore the tangent of the natural angle of sight, to a radius equal to the distance from the highest point of the swell of the muzzle or muzzle band, to the plane passing through the rear of the base ring.

"By *range* is commonly meant the distance between the piece and the object which the ball is intended to strike; or, the first graze of the ball upon the horizontal plane on which the carriage stands. *Point-blank range* is the distance between the piece and the point-blank. *Extreme range* is the distance between the piece and the spot where the ball finally rests.

"*Theory of pointing.*—The *point-blank* is the second point of intersection of the trajectory, or curve described by the projectile in its flight with the line of sight. As the angle of sight is increased, the projectile is thrown farther above the line of sight, and the trajectory and point blank distance become more extended.

"The point-blank range increases with the *velocity*, the *diameter*, and the *density* of the ball. It is also affected by the inclination of the line of sight; but with the angles of elevation used in field service, this effect is too small to be taken into account.

"A piece is said to be aimed *point-blank* when the line of metal, which is the natural line of sight, is directed upon the object. This must be the case when the object is at point-blank distance. When at a greater distance, the pendulum-hausse, or the tangent scale, is raised upon the breech until the sight is at the height which the degree of elevation for the distance may require. An artificial line of sight and an *artificial* point-blank, are thus obtained, and the piece is aimed as before.

"The different lines, angles, &c. which an artilleryman has to take into account in pointing, will be best understood by the following figure:

"A B is the axis of the piece. B I F L is the trajectory, or curve described by the projectile in its flight. C D F is the natural line of sight. C D A is the natural angle of sight.

"The projectile, thrown in the direction of the axis A B D G, is acted upon by the force of gravity, and begins to fall at once below the line at the rate of 16 1/2 feet for one second, 64 1/3 for two, 144 3/4 for three, and so on in proportion to the time. It cuts the line of sight at D, a short distance from the muzzle of the piece and descending, again cuts it at the point F. This second point of intersection is the *point-blank*.

"*Pendulum-hausse*.—The instrument at present in most general use in pointing field-guns at objects beyond the natural point-blank, is called a *pendulum-hausse*, of which the component parts are denominated the *scale*, the *slider*, and the *seat*. The *scale* is made of sheet-brass: at the lower end is a brass bulb filled with lead. The *slider* is of thin brass, and is retained in any desired position on the scale by means of a brass set screw with a milled head. The scale is passed through a slit in a piece of steel, with which it is connected by a brass screw, forming a pivot on which the scale can vibrate laterally: this slit is made long enough to allow the scale to take a vertical position in any *ordinary* cases of inequality of the ground on which the wheels of the carriage may stand. The ends of this piece of steel form two journals, by means of which the scale is supported on the *seat* attached to the piece, and is at liberty to vibrate in the direction of the axis of the piece. The *seat* is of iron, and is fastened to the base of the breech by three screws, in such manner that the centres of the two journal notches shall be at a distance from the axis equal to the radius of the base ring.

"A *muzzle sight* of iron is screwed into the swell of the muzzle of *guns*, or into the middle of the muzzle ring of *howitzers*. The height of this sight is equal to the *dispart* of the piece, so that a line from the *top* of the muzzle sight to the *pivot* of the scale is parallel to the axis of the piece. Consequently the vertical plane of sight passing through the centre line of the scale and the top of the muzzle sight will be also parallel to the axis in any position of the piece: the scale will therefore always indicate correctly the angle which the line of sight makes with the axis. The *seat* for suspending the hausse upon the piece is adapted to each piece according to the varying inclination of the base of the breech to the axis. The *hausse*, the *seat*, and the *muzzle sight*, varying as they do, in their construction and arrangement, according to the configuration of the piece upon which they are intended to be used, are marked for the kind of piece to which they belong. The graduations on the scale are the tangents of each quarter of a degree, to a radius equal to the distance between the muzzle sight and the centre of the journal-notches, which are, in all cases, one inch in rear of the base ring.

"The hausse, when not in use, is carried by the gunner in a leather pouch, suspended from a shoulder-strap.

"PRACTICAL HINTS ON POINTING.

"As it is impossible to point a piece correctly without knowing the *distance* of the object, artillerymen should be frequently practiced in estimating distances by the eye alone, and verifying the estimate afterwards, either by pacing the distance, or by actual measurement with a tape-line or chain, until they acquire the habit of estimating them correctly.

"*Shells* are intended to burst *in* the object aimed at: *spherical case shot* are intended to burst from fifty to seventy-five yards short of it.

"Shell or spherical case firing, for long ranges, is less accurate than that of solid shot.

"At high elevations a solid shot will range farther than a shell or spherical case shot of the same diameter fired with an equal charge. But at low elevations, the shell or spherical case will have a greater initial velocity, and a longer range. If, however, the charges be proportioned to the weights of the projectiles, the solid shot will in all cases have the longest range.

"The velocity or range of a shot is not affected in any appreciable degree by checking the recoil of the carriage, by using a tight wad, or by different degrees of ramming.

"The principal causes which disturb the true flight of the projectile may be simply stated as follows:

"1st. If the wheels of the carriage are not upon the same horizontal plane, the projectile will deviate towards the *lowest* side of the carriage.

"2d. If the direction of the wind is across the line of fire, deviations in the flight of the projectile will be occasioned and in proportion to the strength of the wind, the angle its direction makes with the line of fire, and the velocity of the projectile.

"3d. If the centre of gravity of the projectile be not coincident with the centre of figure, the projectile will deviate towards the *heaviest side*, that is, in the same direction that the centre of gravity of the projectile, while resting in the piece, lies with regard to the centre of figure. Therefore, if a shot be placed in the piece so that its centre of gravity is to the *right* of the centre of the ball, the shot will deviate towards the *right*; and vice versa. If the centre of gravity be above the centre of figure, the range will be *increased*; if *below*, it will be diminished.

"Should an enemy's cavalry be at a distance of 1000 yards from the battery it is about to charge, it will move over the first 400 yards at a walk, approaching to a gentle trot, in about four and a half minutes; it passes over the next 400 yards at a round trot, in a little more than two minutes; and over the last 200 yards at a gallop, in about half a minute, the passage over the whole distance requiring about seven minutes. This estimate will generally be very near the truth, as the ground is not always even, nor easy to move over. Many losses arise from the fire of the artillery and from accidents, and the forming and filling up of intervals create disorder; all of which contribute to retard the charge. Now, a piece can throw, with sufficient deliberation for pointing, two solid shot or three canisters per minute, Each piece of the battery, therefore, might fire nine rounds of solid shot upon the cavalry whilst it is passing over the first 400 yards; two rounds of solid shot and three of canister whilst it is passing over the next 400 yards; and two rounds of canister whilst it is passing over the last 200 yards,—making a total from each gun of eleven round shot and five canisters. To this is added the fire of the supporting infantry.

"Care should be taken not to cease firing solid shot too soon, in order to commence with canister. If the effect of the latter be very great on hard, horizontal, or smooth ground, which is without obstruction of any kind, it is less on irregular and soft ground, or on that covered with brushwood; for, if the ground be not favorable, a large portion of the canister shot is intercepted. A solid shot is true to its direction, and, in ricochet, may hit the second line if it misses the first.

"Solid shot should be used from 350 yards upwards: the use of canister should begin at 350 yards, and the rapidity of the fire increase as the range diminishes. In emergencies, double charges of canister may be used at 150 or 160 yards, with a single cartridge.

"Spherical case ought not, as a general rule, to be used for a less range than 500 yards; and neither spherical case nor shells should be fired at rapidly advancing bodies, as, for instance, cavalry charging.

"The fire of spherical case and of shells on bodies of cavalry in line or column, and in position, is often very effective. To the destructive effects of the projectiles are added the confusion and disorder occasioned amongst the horses by the noise of their explosion; but neither shells nor spherical case should be fired so rapidly as solid shot.

"In case of necessity, solid shot may be fired from howitzers."

654. In the use of small arms, greater accuracy is necessary in the estimation of distances; and no one can fire accurately without knowing the correct distance. Soldiers should practise estimating distances. The stadium, represented in "Target Practice," is an instrument intended to measure distances. Every soldier can readily make his own stadium, that will answer the purpose, by using a small stick of hard wood, or bone, or even his screw-driver, and graduating it for the purpose. The following diagram will explain the principle:

655. A is the eye, B is the hand extended to the full length of the arm, and holding the instrument to be graduated, C is a man of medium height.

Place the man first at fifty yards, and measure his height on the stick B, and mark it; then place him at one hundred yards, and another mark will be obtained: and so on for the principal distances. Each new position will give a new mark on the scale, and the height of the man will measure smaller every time he is removed farther away. The arm must always be extended to the full length, and the stick must always be used to measure the height of a man, or some object known to be about the same height.

656. In estimating distances by the difference in appearance of the same object at different distances, no fixed rules can be laid down, as the eyesight differs materially in different persons. The only way is for each individual to fix his own rules by closely observing the appearance of the same object at known distances. Thus, at one distance, he is able to recognize a man's face and all the details of his dress; a little farther, and he is only able to recognize certain prominent features; still farther, he will be able to distinguish a human figure, but is unable to say whether it is male or female. Practice will soon enable one to judge very correctly, by the various changes in the appearance of the human form, how far it is away.

657. The color of the objects, the condition of the atmosphere, and the formation of the ground affect the estimate of distances very materially. Bright, positive colors seem closer, and neutral colors more

distant; green fields will, therefore, appear closer than ploughed fields. In clear weather, with the sun behind the viewer, objects appear nearer than in dark, cloudy weather, at twilight, by the light of the moon, or dusty or foggy weather. Where the ground is broken, the objects appear larger than on a level plain, and large objects of one color seem to diminish the distance.

658. Tall objects seem closer than lower ones; looking down, objects seem shorter than when looking up. A good eye of ordinary capacity will distinguish the shingles on a house at two hundred and fifty to three hundred yards, in clear weather.

At six hundred to eight hundred yards, the cross-bars of the windows are still visible.

At twelve hundred to fifteen hundred yards, single beams, individual trees, guide-posts, &c. are still seen.

At two thousand five hundred to three thousand yards, large trees are still visible.

At four thousand to five thousand yards, the chimneys are still in sight on the housetops.

At two to three miles, ordinary dwelling-houses are recognized; and churches and windmills are recognizable from six to nine miles.

659. At two thousand yards, a line of infantry looks like a black line, with a bright line over it; cavalry seems a thicker line, with the upper edge broken or notched. The movements can be recognized.

At twelve hundred to fifteen hundred yards, cavalry can be distinguished readily from infantry; the ranks of the latter are visible at twelve hundreds yards.

At one thousand yards, the line of the heads and the motions of the legs of men of the infantry are visible, and the horses' heads of cavalry can be distinguished.

At eight hundred yards, the upper outline of the men are visible of infantry, and, if cavalry, you can distinguish the motions of the horses' legs.

At six hundred yards, men and horses are distinctly visible, but colors are not distinguishable, except white; the kind of head-dress can be recognized.

At four hundred yards, the ornaments are visible on the head-dress, and colors are distinguishable.

At two hundred yards, the men's heads are distinctly visible.

At one hundred and fifty to two hundred yards, you can see the line of the men's eyes.

At eighty yards, the men's eyes are distinct points.

At twenty-five to thirty yards, you can see the white of the eye.

660. Sound travels at the rate of one thousand and eighty-five feet per second, and the difference of time between the flash and the report of a gun will give the distance. On a still night, troops moving at a route step can be heard from five to six

hundred yards; when keeping step, from seven hundred and fifty to eight hundred yards. A troop of horse, at a walk, seven hundred to eight hundred yards; at a gallop or trot, one thousand yards. In stormy weather, the human voice cannot be heard over eighty yards.

661. In firing, men should drop the muzzle of the musket below the object and obtain the correct sight by raising it again. Men are very liable to overshoot firing down hill, and are much more liable to hit firing up hill. Where the hill is steeper than forty-five degrees, men will overshoot, even if they aim at the feet, if the distance is one hundred yards or more.

BATTLE.

662. In battle, men are apt to lose their self possession, and do very absurd things. They rarely take good aim, unless they have been in battles before. Raw troops are liable to panics, and become completely uncontrollable; and this will happen sometimes to veterans.

663. Soldiers are liable to think, when the tide of battle goes against them in that portion of the field where they are engaged, that the whole army has been beaten, and they are liable to give up or run away; and stragglers to the rear frequently report a disastrous defeat, where a victory has been gained.

Such misconceptions are subsequently a great reproach to them, and should, therefore, be guarded against as much as possible; and surrender or retreat should not be thought of until there is no longer any doubt about the result.

RANK.

664. Rank in our service is indicated by the shoulder-strap. Navy officers have an assimilated rank, indicated in the same way. Soldiers should know how to distinguish army and navy officers, in order that they may pay them the proper compliments. The following diagrams show the corresponding grades in each service :—

Lieutenant-General, or Major-General commanding the Army.

ARMY.

Major-General.

Brigadier-General.

NAVY.

Admiral.

Commodore.

ARMY. NAVY.

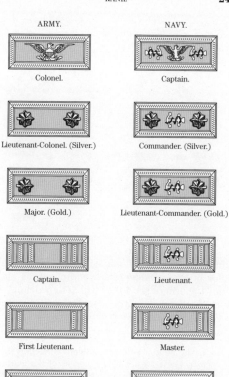

Colonel.

Captain.

Lieutenant-Colonel. (Silver.)

Commander. (Silver.)

Major. (Gold.)

Lieutenant-Commander. (Gold.)

Captain.

Lieutenant.

First Lieutenant.

Master.

Second Lieutenant.

Ensign.

Medical Cadet—a strap of green cloth, with stripe of gold lace three inches long and half an inch wide placed in the middle. (Reg. 1576.)

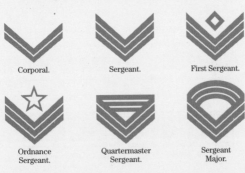

Corporal.   Sergeant.   First Sergeant.

Ordnance Sergeant.   Quartermaster Sergeant.   Sergeant Major.

665. Rank of non-commissioned officers is indicated by the chevrons which they wear, and which are familiar to almost every soldier. The color of the shoulder-straps and chevrons indicates the arm of service to which they belong.—*dark blue* for infantry, *red* for artillery, and *yellow* for cavalry. The following are the Regulations,—viz.:

"Chevrons.

"1577. The rank of non-commissioned officers will be marked by chevrons upon both sleeves of the uniform coat and overcoat, above the elbow, of silk or worsted binding one-half an inch wide, same color as the edging on the coat, points down, as follows:—

"1578. *For a sergeant major*—three bars and an arc, in silk.

"1579. *For a quartermaster sergeant*—three bars and a tie, in silk.

"1580. *For an ordnance sergeant*—three bars and a star, in silk.

"1581. *For a hospital steward*—a half chevron of the following description,—viz.: of emerald green cloth, one and three-fourths inches wide, running obliquely downward from the outer to the inner seam of the sleeve, and at an angle of about thirty degrees with a horizontal, parallel to, and one-eighth of an inch distant from, both the upper and lower edge, an embroidery of yellow silk, one-eighth of an inch wide, and in the centre a "caduceus" two inches long, embroidered also with yellow silk, the head toward the outer seam of the sleeve.

"1582. *For a first sergeant*—three bars and a lozenge, in worsted.

"1583. *For a sergeant*—three bars, in worsted.

"1584. *For a corporal*—two bars, in worsted.

"1585. *For a pioneer*—two crossed hatchets of cloth, same color and material as the edging of the collar, to be sewed on each arm above the elbow in the place indicated for a chevron (those of a corporal to be just above and resting on the chevron), the head of the hatchet upward, its edge outward, of the following dimensions, viz.: *Handle*—four and one-half inches long, one-fourth to one-third of an inch wide. *Hatchet*—two inches long, one inch wide at the edge.

"1586. *To indicate service.*—All non-commissioned officers, musicians, and privates, who have served faithfully for the term of five years, will wear, as a mark of distinction, upon both sleeves of the uniform coat, below the elbow, a diagonal half chevron, one-half an inch wide, extending from seam to seam, the front end nearest the cuff, and one-half an inch above the point of the cuff, to be of the same color as the edging on the coat. In like manner, an additional half chevron, above and parallel to the first, for every subsequent five years of faithful service; distance between each chevron one-fourth of an inch. Service in war will be indicated by a light or sky-blue stripe on each side of the chevron for artillery, and a red stripe for all other corps, the stripe to be one-eighth of an inch wide."

BADGES.

666. Badges are now in use in the Army of the Potomac, and they are an important feature in its organization. The design of the badges is based upon a system of flags now in use in that army for designating the various corps, divisions, and brigades.

667. The badge indicates at once what command the wearer belongs to. The troops are required to wear them and keep them in sight, so that it is not necessary to ask an officer or soldier where he belongs.

668 Every soldier should make himself acquainted with the flags and badges of the army he belongs to. As orderly, he will be required to know them and it is important that soldiers should be able to identify the commands to which their comrades belong.

669. Corps flags are swallow-tails, with the num-

ber of the corps in the centre. Division flags are square, with the badge of the corps in the centre, and the number of the division is indicated by the color. Brigade flags are triangular, with the badge in the centre; and the number of the brigade is indicated by a corresponding arrangement of colors to that of the division.

TAKE CARE OF YOUR HEALTH.

670. The following extracts are from the Sanitary Commission, Dr. Hall's and other advice to soldiers:—

"1. In any ordinary campaign, sickness disables or destroys three times as many as the sword.

"2. Sunstroke may be prevented by wearing a silk handkerchief in the crown of the hat, by a wet cloth, or by moistened green leaves or grass.

"3. Never lie or sit down on the grass or bare earth for a moment; rather use your hat: a handkerchief, even, is a protection. The warmer you are, the greater need of precaution, as a damp vapor is immediately generated, to be absorbed by the clothing, and to cool you off too rapidly.

"4. While marching, or on active duty, the more thirsty you are, the more essential is it to safety of life itself to rinse out the mouth two or three times, and then take a swallow of water at a time, with short intervals. A brave French general, on a forced march, fell dead on the instant by drinking largely of cold water, when snow was on the ground.

"5. Abundant sleep is essential to bodily efficiency, and to that alertness of mind which is all-important in engagement. Few things more certainly and more effectually prevent sound sleep than eating heartily after sundown, especially after a heavy march or desperate battle.

"6. Nothing is more certain to secure endurance and capability of long-continued effort than the avoidance of every thing as a drink except cold water (and coffee at breakfast) Drink as little as possible of even cold water. Experience teaches old soldiers that the less they drink on a march the better, and that they suffer less in the end by controlling the desire to drink, however urgent.

"7. After any sort of exhausting effort, a cup of coffee or tea, hot or cold, is an admirable sustainer of the strength until nature begins to recover herself.

"8. Never eat heartily just before a great undertaking, because the nervous power is irresistibly drawn to the stomach to manage the food eaten, thus draining off that supply which the brain and muscles so much need.

"9. 'Bread and soup are the great items of a soldier's diet in every situation: to make them well is an essential part of his instruction. These great scourges of camp, scurvy and diarrhœ more frequently result from want or skill in cooking than from any other cause whatever. Officers in command, and, more immediately, regimental officers, will, therefore, give strict attention to this vital branch of interior economy.'—WINFIELD SCOTT.

"10. If you will drink spirits, it is incomparably safer to do so *after* an effort than before, for it gives only transient strength, lasting but a few minutes. As it can never be known how long any given effort is to last,—and, if longer than a few minutes, the body becomes more feeble than it would have been without the stimulus,—it is clear that the use *before* an effort is hazardous, and is unwise.

"11. Always eat at regular hours. Neglect in this tends to indigestion, diarrhœa, &c.

"12. Stew or boil your meat, always. Roasting and frying are wasteful and unhealthy modes for camp cooking (particularly frying).

"13. An old soldier drinks and eats as little as possible whilst marching. The recruit, on the contrary, is continually munching the contents of his haversack, and using his canteen; it is a bad habit, and causes more suffering in the end.

"14. Never go to sleep, especially after a great effort, even in hot weather, without some covering over you.

"15. Rather than lie down on the bare ground, lie in the hollow of two logs placed together, or across several smaller pieces of wood laid side by side; or sit on your hat, leaning against a tree. A nap of ten or fifteen minutes in that position will refresh you more than an hour on the bare earth, with the additional advantage of perfect safety.

"16. A *cut* is less dangerous than a bullet-wound, and heals more rapidly.

"17. If from any wound the blood spirts out in jets, instead of a steady stream, you will die in a few minutes, unless it be remedied; because an artery has been divided, and that takes the blood direct from the fountain of life. To stop this instantly, tie a handkerchief or other cloth very loosely BETWEEN the wound and the heart, put a stick, bayonet, or ramrod *between* the skin and the handkerchief, and twist it around until the bleeding ceases, and keep it thus until the surgeon arrives.

"18, If the blood flows in a slow, regular stream, a vein has been pierced, and the handkerchief must be on the other side of the wound from the heart, that is, below the wound.

"19. *Fire low.*—A bullet through the abdomen (belly or stomach) is more certainly fatal than if aimed at the head or heart; for in the latter cases the ball is often glanced off by the bone, or follows round it under the skin. But when it enters the stomach or bowels, from any direction, death is inevitable, but scarcely ever instantaneous. Generally the person lives a day or two, with perfect clearness of intellect, often *not* suffering greatly. The practical bearing of this statement in reference to the future is clear. *Fire low.*

"20. Whenever possible, take a plunge into any lake or running stream every morning, as soon as you get up; if none at hand, endeavor to wash the body all over, as soon as you leave your bed: for personal cleanliness acts like a charm against all diseases, always either warding them off altogether, or greatly mitigating their severity and shortening their duration.

"21. Keep the hair of the head closely cut, say within an inch and a half of the scalp in every part, repeated on the first of each month, and wash the whole scalp plentifully in cold water every morning.

"22. Wear woollen stockings and moderately loose shoes, keeping the toe and finger nails cut close. Wash the stockings whenever soiled and the underclothing once a week. Thoroughly dry both.

"23. It is important to wash the feet well every night (not in the morning); because it aids to keep the skin and nails soft, to prevent chafings, blisters, and corns, all of which greatly interfere with a soldier's duty.

"24. If the feet begin to chafe, rub the socks with common soap where they come in contact with the sore places. If you rub the feet well with soap (hard soap) before the march, you will scarcely be troubled with sore feet.

"25. The most universally safe position, after all stunnings, hurts, and wounds, is that of being placed on the back, the head being elevated three or four inches only,—aiding, more than any thing else can do, to equalize and restore the proper circulation of the blood.

"26. The more weary you are after a march or other work, the more easily will you take cold, if you remain still, after it is over, unless the moment you cease motion you throw a coat or blanket over your shoulders. This precaution should be taken in the warmest weather, especially if there is even a slight air stirring.

"27. The greatest physical kindness you can show a severely wounded comrade is, first to place him on his back, and then give him some water to drink from a canteen or ambulance-bucket. I have seen a dying man clutch at a single drop of water from the finger's end, with the voraciousness of a famished tiger.

"28. If wet to the skin by rain or swimming rivers, keep in motion until the clothes are dried; and no harm will result.

"29. Whenever it is possible, do, by all means, when you have to use water for cooking or drinking from ponds or sluggish streams, boil it well, and, when cool, shake it, or stir it, so that the oxygen of the air shall get to it, which greatly improves it for drinking. This boiling arrests the process of fermentation, which arises from the presence of organic and inorganic impurities, thus tending to prevent cholera and all bowel-diseases. If there is no time for boiling, at least strain it through a cloth, even if you have to use a shirt or trowsers-leg.

"30. Water can be made almost ice-cool in the hottest weather, by closely enveloping a filled canteen, or other vessel, with woollen cloth kept plentifully wetted and exposed.

"31. While on a march, lie down the moment you halt for a rest. Every minute spent in that position refreshes more than five minutes standing or loitering about.

"32. A daily evacuation of the bowels is indispensable to bodily health vigor, and endurance: this is promoted, in many cases, by stirring a tablespoonful of corn (Indian) meal in a glass of water, and drinking it on rising in the morning.

"33. Inattention to nature's calls is a frequent source of disease. The strictest discipline in the performance of these duties is absolutely essential to health, as well as to decency. Men should never be allowed to void their excrement elsewhere than in the regular-established sinks. In well-regulated camps the sinks are visited daily by a police party, a layer of earth thrown in, and lime and other disinfecting agents employed to prevent them from becoming offensive and unhealthy. It is the duty of the surgeon to call the attention of the commanding officer to any neglect of this important item of camp police, to see that the shambles, where the cattle are slaughtered, are not allowed to become offensive, and that all offal is promptly buried at a sufficient distance from camp, and covered by at least four feet of earth.

"34. The *site of a camp* should be selected for the *dryness of its soil, its proximity to fresh water of good quality*, and *shelter from high winds*. It should be on a slight declivity, in order to facilitate drainage, and not in the vicinity of swamps or stagnant water. A trench at least eight inches deep should be dug around each tent, to secure dryness, and these should lead into other and deeper main drains or gutters, by which the water will be conducted away from the tents.

"35. The tents for the men should be placed as far from each other as the 'Regulations' and the dimensions of the camp permit (never less than two paces). Crowding is always injurious to health. No refuse, slops, or excrement should be allowed to be deposited in the trenches for drainage around the tents. Each tent should be thoroughly swept out daily, and the materials used for bedding aired and sunned, if possible. The canvas should be raised freely at its base, and it should be kept open as much as possible during the daytime, in dry weather, in order to secure ventilation; for tents are liable to become very unhealthy if not constantly and thoroughly aired. Free ventilation of tents should be secured at night, by opening and raising the base of the tent to as great an extent as the weather will permit.

"36. The crowding of men in tents for sleeping is highly injurious to health, and will always be prevented by a commanding officer who is anxious for the welfare of his men. Experience has proved that sleeping beneath simple sheds of canvas, or even in the open air, is less dangerous to health than overcrowding in tents.

"37. The men should sleep in their shirts and drawers, removing the shoes, stockings, and outer clothing, except when absolutely impracticable. Sleeping in the clothes is never so refreshing, and is absolutely unhealthy.

"38. *Loose bowels*, namely, acting more than once a day, with a feeling of debility afterwards, is the first step towards cholera. The best remedy is instant and perfect quietude of body, eating nothing but boiled rice, with or without boiled milk. In more decided cases, a woolen flannel, with two thicknesses in front, should be bound tightly around the abdomen, especially if marching is a necessity.

"To have 'been to the wars' is a life-long honor, in-creasing with advancing years; while to have died in defence of your country will be the boast and glory of your children's children."

COOKING.

671. THE ration allowed the soldier is large enough, and its component parts are sufficiently variable, to admit of a great variety of very palatable dishes: and it is only necessary to refer to some of the numerous cook-books to be had, to make them, where the situation of the troops is such that they can avail themselves of the requisite cooking-utensils.

672. The cooking-utensils issued to troops are, however, so limited, that very little variety is practicable. The mess-pans and camp-kettles are all that are furnished the soldier. Of these, the mess-pan is not available for cooking, and is only useful to serve up the food after being cooked. Frying-pans, tin cups, plates, knives and forks, &c., are sometimes issued to volunteers by State authorities on entering service, but are not subsequently furnished, and, when worn out or lost, must be replaced by means of the company fund.

673. Hence, instructions for cooking in the field must be adapted to the means within the soldier's reach, and such makeshifts as experience has sug-

gested. At permanent camps and garrisons, the cooking can be carried to the perfection of that of a hotel, by a judicious management of the company savings, or contributions from other sources. No care is so well rewarded as that which is devoted to making the most of the ration and presenting to the men the best possible diet that can be made of it.

674. BREAD is issued to the soldier either as baker's bread, hard bread, flour, or corn meal. The first two require no further preparation; the last two must be prepared.

675. *Bread*, such as is usually made by bakers, can be had only when the troops are stationary, unless there is a baker in the command and the men have experience in making ovens. If kept more than two or three days, it becomes dry and unpalatable. It is too bulky for the march.

676. *Hard bread*, although not so bulky as soft bread, is still inconvenient when required to be transported in quantity. Three days' rations fill a soldier's haversack. When old, it is unpalatable, and sometimes indigestible. It can be made more agreeable to the taste by toasting, either in a dry condition, or soaked in water for a few moments. Crumbs of hard bread may be made very palatable by soaking them in water, and then frying them in a pan with a little pork fat. Hard bread soon spoils when it gets wet, and must be used immediately, or it will be worthless.

677. *Flour* is more portable than bread; but without experience in cooking, with the limited means at their disposal, soldiers are liable to make a very indigestable bread from it. Where troops halt for a few days, it is economical to build small ovens of clay, which may be made with great facility after a little experience. A *ferment* is always necessary to make light palatable bread of flour. A stock of ferment may be kept constantly on hand by retaining a piece of dough from one baking to another; and it is best transported by packing it in the flour.

678. The simplest and best method is to make self-rising flour, by incorporating with the flour, in a dry state, bicarbonate of soda and acid phosphate of lime. These articles must be finely pulverized and minutely incorporated with the flour. A comparatively small quantity is required. A dollar's worth is sufficient for a barrel of flour. The self-rising flour, so well known and highly prized in the mining-districts of California, is made in this way. It requires only the addition of salt and sufficient water to make a dough, and can be baked in the ashes between the halves of an old canteen, or even rolled up in wet paper or covered with leaves. It is equally good for pancakes or fritters. These last may be made much more digestible by the addition of boiled rice.

679. *Corn meal* is much more available for troops in the field where it can be obtained fresh, as it requires no ferment, and requires no cooking-

utensils,—a plain board placed before a fire being all the oven absolutely necessary. With a frying-pan, thin cakes can be rapidly baked, and are an excellent diet. The meal can always be had fresh by transporting the small hand-mill in common use.

680. An excellent substitute for bread, when the usual ration cannot be had, is parched wheat, or parched corn, either eaten in the grain, or ground into flour. It is more healthy than the ordinary bread; and the flour, mixed with water, either cold or hot, is much more palatable than from its crudity would be supposed. Boiled with meat, it is an excellent substitute for vegetables. Boiled wheat and boiled corn,—the latter usually called hominy—are available almost everywhere, when bread cannot be had.

681. MEAT is issued to soldiers in the form of fresh beef, salt beef, salt pork, and bacon. Fresh beef is perishable, as well as bulky, and, where it accompanies troops on the hoof, requires time to slaughter and to cook. Salt beef is bulky, but less perishable than fresh. Salt pork and bacon are preferred by old troops on the march, as being the least bulky, easily cooked, and more readily kept than beef. It has, however, been found by experience best to alternate those different kinds according to means and opportunities.

682. *Fresh beef* is most economically cooked by boiling in the camp-kettles usually furnished, particularly when the cooking is for the entire com-

pany, as the liquor in which the beef has been cooked is then used for soup. The value of soup is not fully appreciated by the American soldier. It is the most nourishing and healthy diet that can be prepared from his ration, and enables the mixed vegetables to be used in a palatable form.

683. In boiling beef to make soup, the proportion of water should be about a quart to the pound, the meat being cut in such a shape that it will be covered by the water. It should be made to boil as soon as possible, and then the fire should be reduced so as to let the pot simmer. From three to four hours are necessary to cook the beef. The soup may be made at the same time, if necessary, or the liquor may be saved from one day to another. It keeps best in earthen vessels, where they can be had for the purpose.

684. The bones of beef are the best for making soup, and should always be saved for that purpose. Soldiers, however, are apt to throw them away, particularly where the messes are small and the amount does not seem to justify the economy.

685. Roasting beef is impracticable in the field, but broiling it is the common practice. It is a healthy but wasteful mode of cooking. Placed on the coals, or stuck upon a stick over the fire, it is easily cooked, and very palatable. Frying, particularly in fat, is neither economical nor healthy, although a very common practice in the service. The gravy is used as a substitute for butter.

686. *Salt beef* can be cooked in but one way to advantage; and that is, by boiling. It should be thoroughly soaked in cold water (cold water dissolves salt better than warm water), and frequently changed, for ten or twelve hours, or longer, and should then be cooked the same as fresh beef. It requires longer to cook than fresh beef, and is not available for soup, on account of the salt it contains. When old, it must be cooked a long time to be rendered palatable. When very salt, it may be added to potatoes and onions, and a palatable hash made of it.

687. *Salt pork* is usually boiled. As with salt beef, it should be well soaked to extract the salt, and then boiled for three or four hours. The grease, which should be skimmed off and saved, may be used in various ways as a substitute for lard: in the field, however, this cannot well be done. In permanent camps and garrison it can he saved, and, if not used, can be sold to advantage and will serve to increase the company fund. When issued to small messes, salt pork, like fresh beef, can be broiled on the coals; but this is a very wasteful method of preparing it.

688. *Bacon* is usually cooked in the same way as salt pork. It is, generally, not so salt, but requires to be well washed and scraped of the rust to make it palatable. Frying salt pork and bacon has the same objections as frying fresh beef. In an emergency, salt pork or bacon may be eaten without

cooking, or it may be cooked and eaten cold,—
which is preferable. Cutting it in thin slices and
broiling it on the coals rapidly, varies the taste
when the appetite grows tired of it boiled or raw.

689. *Beans* and *peas* form a very nutritious diet.
They require considerable time to cook, and, therefore, are not available on the march. They should
be soaked over-night, and boiled slowly for six or
eight hours. Salt should not be added until the
beans are nearly done. The water in which they are
cooked should be soft. Soup is the only available
dish in the field, except plain boiling. Baked pork
and beans can only be had with the necessary conveniences. A piece of pork or bacon should be
added to the pot when boiling bean soup. About
two pounds to the gallon is a good proportion.

690. *Rice* is not fully appreciated by the Northern
soldier, and the cooking is rarely well done. Some
experience is necessary to cook it well. When well
cooked, each grain of rice will be separate and dry.
When badly cooked, it forms an unpalatable paste.
Two quarts of water to half a pound of rice, well
washed. It should boil for about ten minutes, or until
the grains of rice begin to swell and soften. The
water should then be poured off, the pot closely covered and set near the fire,—but not too close, or it
will scorch. In twenty minutes the grains will have
swelled to their fullest extent and the rice be done.
Each grain will be separate and dry; and the rice
may be eaten with sugar, molasses, or beef-gravy.

The Chinese live almost exclusively on rice, and perform arduous labors with no other diet.

691. *Hominy* may be issued in lieu of rice, and is cooked very much in the same way. It requires to be boiled about an hour; and great care must be taken to prevent it from scorching. In all cooking it should be remembered that water cannot be heated in an ordinary kettle beyond 212∞. After it commences to boil, it cannot be made any hotter; any increase of fire is only calculated to burn the victuals, and does not hasten the cooking. The mechanical ebullition of water sometimes facilitates the cooking of some dishes, but not in consequence of any increase of heat to the water. Scorching of rice or hominy, or any other food, in the thin camp-kettles, is very liable to occur, and may easily be prevented by using a false bottom in the kettle, which may be made either of wood, or tin, or sheet iron. Salt and pepper are the best condiments for hominy. What is left over may be cut in slices, and fried in bacon or pork fat, and makes a good dish. Mush made of corn meal may be fried in the same way.

692. *Coffee* is the soldier's greatest sustainer; and he will miss it more than any other part of his ration. When issued in the grain, great care is necessary in roasting it. The pan in which it is roasted should be slightly greased, to prevent scorching. A steady fire should be maintained, and the coffee constantly stirred. Roasted coffee in the grain is not so good as

green, as it deteriorates after roasting the longer it is kept, and still more so after being ground. Coffee should be boiled about twenty minutes, and is better when made in large quantity for the entire company. There is economy in adding the proper proportion of sugar for the whole amount of coffee whilst cooking. After the coffee is sufficiently cooked, a cup of cold water should be added, and, by allowing it to stand a few minutes, the grounds all settle at the bottom. Experience will teach how coffee should be used: strong coffee will be found to be very injurious to some persons and very salutary to others.

693. *Tea* may be issued in lieu of coffee, but is not so much preferred, although equally valuable to the soldier in its qualities. On a long and fatiguing march a canteen of cold tea is invaluable, greatly relieving exhaustion. The secret of making tea consists in using vessels that are entirely free from any thing that can affect the natural taste of the tea. The kettle, if not used exclusively for tea, should, therefore, be thoroughly scoured each time before using. The water should first be made to boil; the tea is then added, and allowed to boil for a few seconds, then removed from the fire, and the kettle is covered closely and allowed to stand for five minutes. It is then ready for use. The proportions in which coffee and tea are used are limited to the allowance: a ration is deemed sufficient to make coffee or tea for two meals daily.

694. *Desiccated vegetables* are not appreciated, because the cooking is not understood. The practice of drying vegetables in the green state, for winter use, is well understood and practised by the peasantry of Europe, although not equal to the practice of canning in this country. Vegetables of this kind have the advantage in portability, and are great health-preservers where fresh vegetables cannot be had. When well cooked, they are very palatable. They require to be soaked several hours, and should be cooked about three hours. No salt or pepper is required, as sufficient has already been added to preserve them. They swell greatly; and care should be taken not to add too much to the quantity of water. As soup, they are most palatable. An ounce of vegetables to a quart of water is a good proportion. Rice, fresh potatoes, and onions, if they can be had, improve the soup.

695. *Desiccated potatoes* are best cooked by adding sufficient water to cover the potatoes, and then boiling slowly until all the water is evaporated, leaving a dry mush that is a very good substitute for fresh potatoes.

696. *Potatoes* are much injured by bad cooking. It should be remembered that potatoes, like any other food, are done at a certain time, and that any further cooking is not only unnecessary, but injurious. It requires about half an hour to cook them: the time varies a little with the size of the vegetables. After the potatoes have been placed in cold

water and boiled about fifteen minutes, the kettle should be removed from the fire, and the boiling suddenly checked, for five minutes, by pouring in a cup of cold water. The kettle is placed on the fire again and the boiling continued for fifteen minutes longer; the water is then poured off, and the potatoes covered up until served. This principle of checking the boiling can be remembered to advantage in cooking other solids that are liable to be under-done in the water. By checking the heat of the water suddenly, the heat in the potatoes strikes into the centre, and thus aids in cooking it through.

697. *Vinegar*, moderately used, is a great health-preserver in the army. With salt and pepper added to cold meat, and an onion finely cut up, it makes an excellent relish. Stale cold meat, soaked in vinegar, and then stewed with potatoes and onions, makes a kind of ragout hash, that is very palatable. Cabbage, finely cut, with pepper, salt, and vinegar, is more palatable and digestible than when cooked. An excellent warm dressing for cabbage, salad, or cold potatoes sliced, is made by cutting a piece of fat salt pork or bacon in small pieces like dice, and frying out the fat, then adding a good proportion of vinegar when well heated, and pouring it over the salad, previously seasoned with salt and pepper; a sliced onion is a good addition.

698. *Soup*, although not a favorite dish of the American soldier, cannot be too soon adopted, and

the art of making the many varieties studied. It is most easily made in quantity, and is by far the healthiest food that can be prepared in the field. Beef-broth can be used as the basis for nearly all soups: mutton and other meats, and even pork, can be used. By changing the ingredients added to the broth, great variety can be obtained. Rice, mixed desiccated vegetables, pulverized hard bread, vegetables of all kinds, flour, butter, &c. can all be used in a variety of proportions and quantities. An agreeable taste can be given to any soup by adding to it a mixture of scorched flour and fried pork fat. A handful of dry flour should be scorched in one pan, taking care to stir it constantly that it may not burn; the pork fat, cut up into small pieces and fried brown, should be prepared in another pan, and incorporated with the flour whilst hot.

699. The foregoing suggestions are offered, the result of many years' experience, and, it is hoped, will give some idea of what may be done in campaign with the ration. The experience of each soldier will furnish additional aid in sustaining himself on the food furnished. All soldiers cannot avail themselves alike of the same suggestions; but it is hoped that each one will be assisted by what is here laid down.

700. It is a great mistake to suppose that men cannot live without a systematic supply. In a country like ours, teeming with every variety of provisions, it is possible to move through the country and live upon it, unless the number of men in the

command exceeds in a great degree the resources of the country,—which would rarely be the case. The Confederate armies have been living in the main on corn and pork. By carrying along a portable corn-mill for each company, the troops could prepare their own bread; and beef on the hoof, together with what meat can be found in the country, will furnish all that is absolutely necessary to sustain an army for the short periods necessary to accomplish specific results.

701. Even mills are not absolutely necessary where grain can be had; for boiled wheat, and parched corn and wheat, are excellent substitutes for bread. The early settlers of Oregon, before mills could be built, lived upon boiled wheat instead of bread; and Indians and trappers live for months upon parched corn, either in the grain or pulverized, and mixed with meat or fat, or boiled in soup.

702. In war, if a great end can be accomplished by dispensing for a short time with the conveniences of daily life, it shortens the total amount of suffering and deprivation to do so; and commanding officers should not hesitate to dispense with the comforts to which they may be accustomed, and soldiers should endure, without murmuring, what has a tendency to shorten their sufferings in the aggregate.

703. Such utensils as will enable the individual soldier to be independent of all transportation or movement of troops, in the preparation of his food, are what is mainly required. A small iron vessel,

half pan and half kettle, an iron fork, folding on a hinge, with a hook on the handle, to attach to his cooking-vessel to put it on and take it off the fire, and a suitable knife, would seem to be sufficient to enable a soldier to do all the cooking that is absolutely requisite for short campaigns.

704. With strong and well-made little bags for keeping the sugar, coffee, salt, pepper, flour, &c. separate, his pantry, kitchen, and bed-chamber would be wherever he halted for the night; and in such a case, with no waiting for wagons to come up before supper can be had, and none to load up after breakfast, the march of an army would be greatly facilitated. It is the necessity of subsistence that compels armies to move upon certain lines, and prevents them from marching where they choose. Every soldier should make the art of cooking his study: more disease and deaths are occasioned in an army by bad cooking than by any other cause.

705. It may not be out of place here to suggest to soldiers who have been deprived of food for an unusual length of time and are suddenly placed within reach of an abundance of provisions, that by satisfying their hunger at once they are very liable to do themselves a permanent injury. It is recommended to procure first a cup of moderate coffee or tea, and a cracker. After eating this, and allowing an hour or so for the stomach to gain strength from this nourishment, a moderately full meal may be eaten without injury.

ON DETACHED SERVICE.

706. ENLISTED men on detached service, unattended by a commissioned officer, are frequently at a loss how to provide themselves with rations and transportation. The following general principles should be borne in mind under such circumstances.

707. When soldiers are detached from their companies for periods extending beyond a muster-day, they should be accompanied by their descriptive lists and clothing accounts. If this is not done, they cannot be mustered, or paid, or receive clothing, during their absence. It is always best to send descriptive lists, as the exigencies of the service may keep the men away from their companies longer than was originally intended.

708. Soldiers on detached service should always be accompanied by the order detaching them, and showing the duty they are on,—which order it is necessary to present to the commanding officers of posts and districts through which the men are required to pass, who will give the necessary orders in the case for the transportation and rations that they require.

709. Where it is very inconvenient to carry rations, or where they cannot be obtained, the soldiers can purchase their own food at their discretion, and will subsequently be reimbursed by the commutation of the ration. Under any circumstances, where a

soldier does not receive his rations in kind, they can always be commuted at the cost-price of the ration, when due. (See paragraphs 36 and 37).

710. Where, from any circumstance, soldiers find themselves separated or detached from their commands, without the necessary means or authority for rejoining, in order to prevent their being reported as deserters, they should at once report in person to the nearest post or command, and state their case to the commanding officer, whose duty it is to provide for them and have them forwarded to their proper commands at the earliest opportunity.

711. The soldier should bear in mind that any failure to take proper steps to join his command, when separated from it, no matter what the cause, involves inconveniences and troubles that are not overcome without much difficulty. Sickness, insurmountable accidents, &c. all require to be established by conclusive testimony, to free him from the suspicions that always attend an unusual absence from his proper post.

MEDALS.

712. By a resolution of Congress, approved July 12, 1862, the President was authorized to cause two thousand "medals of honor" to be prepared, with suitable emblematic devices, "to be presented to such non-commissioned officers and privates as

shall most distinguish themselves by their gallantry in action and other soldierlike qualities during the present insurrection."

713. This is the only instance in our service of legislation for rewarding soldiers with medals for meritorious services. During the Mexican War, "Certificates of Merit" were given, that insured an increase of pay; and, as a rule, soldiers have generally been rewarded with money or land for extraordinary services.

714. Medals are lasting mementoes of meritorious actions: they survive changes of fortune and station, are cherished with pride and reverence by descendants, and are, therefore, commendable objects of a soldier's ambition. It is well at all times for soldiers to procure certificates from their immediate commander for whatever services they have rendered, and the manner in which they have been performed. It is recommended to enlisted men to provide themselves with a little blank-book, in which such certificates may be entered and preserved.

715. These certificates are particularly valuable to individual soldiers serving on expeditions where their proper companies or regiments are not represented, and where the muster-rolls and reports will fail to show that they participated. Such papers become exceedingly valuable in the lapse of time, and may, in many instances, involve extra pay or pensions.

SOLDIERS' LETTERS.

716. By the 11th section of the act approved July 22, 1861, soldiers are allowed to send letters without prepayment of postage, the postage to be collected on the delivery of the letter. The Post-Office regulations require that such letter shall be endorsed "Soldier's Letter," and signed by the commanding officer or a field officer of the regiment to which the soldier belongs.

PENSIONS.

717. The following are the instructions published by the Pension Office, relative to the manner of procuring pensions by those who are entitled to them. They are plain and simple, and there is no necessity of feeing a lawyer to make out the applications for a pension. Any intelligent soldier can do it himself.

"GENERAL PROVISIONS.

"Under the act of Congress approved July 14, 1862, pensions are granted to the following classes of persons:—

"I. Invalids, disabled since March 4, 1861, in the military or naval service of the United States, in the line of duty.

"II. WIDOWS, of officers, soldiers, or seamen dying of wounds received or of disease contracted in the military or naval service, as above.

"III. CHILDREN, under sixteen years of age, of such deceased persons, if there is no widow surviving, or from the time of the widow's re-marriage.

"IV. MOTHERS of officers, soldiers, or seamen, deceased as aforesaid, provided the latter have left neither widow nor children under sixteen years of age; and provided, also, that the mother was dependent, wholly or in part, upon the deceased for support.

"V. SISTERS, under sixteen years of age, of such deceased persons, dependent on the latter, wholly or in part, for support, provided there are no rightful claimants of either of the three last preceding classes.

"The rates of pension to the several classes and grades are distinctly set forth in the first section of the act. Only one full pension in any case will be allowed to the relatives of a deceased officer, soldier, or seaman, and in order of precedence as set forth above. When more than one minor child or orphan sister thus becomes entitled to pension, the same must be divided equally between them.

"Invalid pensions, under this law, will commence from the date of the pensioner's discharge from service, provided application is made within one year thereafter. If the claim is not made until a later date, the pension will commence from the time of the application. Pensions of widows and minors will commence from the death of the officer, soldier, or seaman on whose service the claim is based.

ARMY PENSIONS.

"*Declarations* (including evidence of identity) are required to be made before a court of record, or before some officer of such court duly authorized to administer oaths, and having custody of its seal. *Testimony* other than that indicated above may be taken before a justice of the peace, or other officer having like authority to administer oaths; but in no case will any evidence be received that is verified before an officer who is concerned in prosecuting the claim, or has a manifest interest therein.

"The subjoined forms, marked, respectively, A, B, C, D, and E, will guide applicants for pensions, of the army branch, in the several classes. The forms should be exactly followed in every instance. No attorney will be regarded as having filed the necessary declaration and affidavits, as contemplated by the sixth and seventh sections of the act, unless the *forms*, as well as the instructions given in this pamphlet, are strictly complied with.

"In support of the allegations made in the claimant's declaration, testimony will be required in accordance with the following rules:—

"1. The claimant's identity must be proved by two witnesses, certified by a judicial officer to be respectable and credible, who are present and witness the signature of the declarant, and who state, upon oath or affirmation, their belief, either from personal acquaintance or for other reasons given, that he or she is the identical person he or she represents himself or herself to be.

"2. Every applicant for an invalid pension must, if in his power, produce the certificate of the captain, or of some other commissioned officer, under whom he served, distinctly stating the time and place of the said applicant's having been wounded or otherwise disabled, and the nature of the disability; and that the said disability arose while he was in the service of the United States and in the line of his duty.

"3. If it be impracticable to obtain such certificate, by reason of the death or removal of said officers, it must be so stated under oath by the applicant, and his averment of the fact proved by persons of known respectability, who must state particularly all the knowledge they may possess in relation to such death or removal; then secondary evidence can be received. In such case the applicant must produce the testimony of at least two credible witnesses (who were in condition to know the facts about which they testify), whose good character must be vouched for by a judicial officer, or by some one known to the department. The witnesses must give a minute narrative of the facts in relation to the matter, and must show how they obtained a knowledge of the facts to which they testify.

"4. The usual certificate of disability for discharge should show the origin, character, and degree of the claimant's disability; but when that is wanting or defective, the applicant will be required to be examined by some surgeon regularly appointed, unless clearly impracticable.

"5. The habits of the applicant, and his occupation since he left the service, should be shown by at least two credible witnesses.

"If the applicant claims a pension as the widow of a deceased officer or soldier, she must prove the legality of her marriage, the death of her husband, and that she is still a widow. She must also furnish the names and ages of decedent's children under sixteen years of age at her husband's decease, and the place of their residence. On a subsequent marriage her pension will cease, and the minor child or children of the deceased officer or soldier, if any be living, under the age of sixteen years, will be entitled to the same in her stead, from the date of such marriage, on the requisite proof, under a new declaration. Proof of the marriage of the parents and of the age of claimants will be required in all applications in behalf of minor children. The legality of the marriage, in either case, may be ascertained by the certificate of the clergyman who joined them in wedlock, or by the testimony of respectable persons having knowledge of the fact, in default of record evidence, which last must always be furnished, or its absence shown. The ages and number of children may be ascertained by the deposition of the mother, accompanied by the testimony of respectable persons having knowledge of them, or by transcripts from the parish or town registers duly authenticated.

"A mother, to be entitled to a pension, as having been wholly or partly dependent on a deceased officer or soldier, must prove that the latter contributed to her support for a certain period, showing specifically in what manner and to what extent.

"If the claimant be a dependent sister, like proof will be required of the marriage of her parents, and of her relationship to the deceased.

"Guardians of minor claimants must, in all cases, produce evidence of their authority as such, under the seal of the court from which their appointment is obtained.

"Applicants of the last four classes enumerated on page 274, who have in any manner aided or abetted the rebellion against the United States Government, are not entitled to the benefits of this act.

"Invalid applicants who are minors may apply in their own behalf, without the intervention of a guardian.

"Attorneys for claimants must have proper authority from those in whose behalf they appear. Powers of attorney must be signed in the presence of two witnesses, and acknowledged before a duly-qualified officer, whose official character must be certified under seal.

"In all cases the post-office address of the claimant must be distinctly stated, over his or her proper signature.

"Applications under this act will be numbered and acknowledged, to be acted on in their turn. In filing additional evidence, correspondents should always give the number of the claim as well as the name of the claimant.

"JOSEPH H. BARRETT,

"*Commissioner*.

"PENSION OFFICE, October 1, 1863."

A.

FORM OF DECLARATION FOR AN INVALID PENSION.

STATE [DISTRICT OR TERRITORY] of ———   } ss.:
            County of ———,

On this ——— day of ———, A.D. one thousand eight hundred and ———, personally appeared before me, ——— [*here state the official character of the person administering the oath*] within and for the county and State aforesaid, A. B., aged ——— years, a resident of ——— in the State of ———, who, being duly sworn according to law, declares that he is the identical ——— who enlisted in the service of the United States at ———, on the ——— day of ———, in the year ———, as a ——— in company———, commanded by ———, in the ——— regiment of ———, in the war of 1861, and was honorably discharged on the ——— day of ———, in the year ———; that while in the service aforesaid, and in the line of his duty, he received the following wound (*or other disability, as the case may be*): [*Here give a particular and minute account of the wound or other injury, and state how, when, and where it occurred, where the applicant has resided since leaving the service, and what has been his occupation.*]

My post-office address is as follows: ————.

(Signature of claimant.)

Also personally appeared ———— and ————, residents of (*county, city, or town*), persons whom I certify to be respectable and entitled to credit, and who, being by me duly sworn, say that they were present and saw ———— sign his name (*or make his mark*) to the foregoing declaration; and they further swear that they have every reason to believe, from the appearance of the applicant and their acquaintance with him, that he is the identical person he represents himself to be; and they further swear that they have no interest in the prosecution of this claim.

(Signatures of witnesses.)

Sworn to and subscribed before me, this ———— day of ————, A.D. 186—; and I hereby certify that I have no interest, direct or indirect, in the prosecution of this claim.

(Signature of judge or other officer.)

B.

FORM OF DECLARATION FOR OBTAINING A WIDOW'S ARMY PENSION.

State [Territory or District] of ———, ⎫
　　　　　　　County of ———, ⎬ *ss.:*

On this ——— day of ———, A.D. ———, personally appeared before me, ——— of the ———, A. B., a resident of ———, and State [Territory or District] of ———, aged ——— years, who, being first duly sworn according to law, doth on her oath make the following declaration, in order to obtain the benefit of the provision made by the act of Congress approved July 14, 1862: That she is the widow of ———, who was a ——— in company ———, commanded by ———, in the ——— regiment of ———, in the war of 1861, who [*here specify the time, place, and cause of death*]. She further declares that she was married to the said ——— on the ——— day of ———, in the year ———; that her husband, the aforesaid ———, died on the day above mentioned, and that she has remained a widow ever since that period (*or, if she has remarried and again become a widow, the fact must be stated*), as will more fully appear by reference to the proof hereto annexed. She also declares that she has not in any manner been engaged in, or aided or abetted, the rebellion in the United States.

My post-office address is as follows: ———.

　　　　　　　　　　(Declarant's signature.)

Also personally appeared ——— and ———, residents of (*county, city, or town*), persons whom I certify to be respectable and entitled to credit, and who, being by me duly sworn, say that they were present and saw ——— sign her name (*or make her mark*) to the foregoing declaration; and they further swear that they have every reason to believe, from the appearance of the applicant and their acquaintance with her, that she is the identical person she represents herself to be, and that they have no interest in the prosecution of this claim.

(Signature of witnesses.)

Sworn to and subscribed before me, this ——— day of ———, A.D. 186—; and I hereby certify that I have no interest, direct or indirect, in the prosecution of this claim.

(Signature of judge or other officer.)

C.

FORM OF DECLARATION FOR MINOR CHILDREN IN ORDER TO OBTAIN ARMY PENSIONS.

State [Territory or District] of ———, } *ss.:*
County of ———,

On this ——— day of ———, A.D. ———, personally appeared before the ——— of the ———, A. B., a resident of ———, in the county of ———, and State [Territory or District] of ———, aged ——— years, who, being first duly sworn according to law, doth on oath make the following declaration, as guardian of the minor child of ——— deceased, in order to obtain the benefits of the provision made by the act of Congress, approved July 14, 1862, granting pensions to minor children, under sixteen years of age, of deceased officers and soldiers; that he is the guardian of ——— [naming the minor child or children, his ward or wards], whose father was a ——— in company ———, commanded by ———, in the ——— regiment of ———, in the war of 1861, and

that the said ——— died at ——— on the ——— day
of ———, in the year ——— [*here state the cause of
death*], that the mother of the child ——— aforesaid died
(or again married, being now the wife of ———) on the
——— day of ——— in the year ———; and that the
date of birth of his said ward—, as follows:

He further declares that the parents of his said ward—
were married at ———, on the ——— day of ———,
in the year ———, by ———.

My post-office address is as follows: ———.

(Guardian's signature.)

Also personally appeared ——— and ———, residents
of (*county, city, or town*), persons whom I certify to be
respectable and entitled to credit, and who, being by me
duly sworn, say that they were present and saw ———
sign ——— name (*or make her mark*) to the foregoing
declaration; and they further swear that they have every
reason to believe, from the appearance of the applicant
and their acquaintance with her, that she is the identical
person she represents herself to be, and that they have
no interest in the prosecution of this claim.

(Signature of witnesses.)

Sworn to and subscribed before me, this ——— day
of ———, A.D. 186—; and I hereby certify that I have
no interest, direct or indirect, in the prosecution of this
claim.

(Signature of judge or other officer.)

D.

FORM OF DECLARATION FOR MOTHER'S APPLICATION FOR ARMY PENSION.

State [Territory or District] of ———,
County of ———, } *ss.:*

On this ——— day of ———, A.D. ———, personally appeared before the ——— of the ———, A. B., a resident of ——— in the county of ———, and State [Territory or District] of———, aged ——— years, who, being first duly sworn according to law, doth on her oath make the following declaration, in order to obtain the benefits of the provisions made by the act of Congress approved July 14, 1862: That she is the widow of ——— —, and mother of ———, who was a ——— in company ———, commanded by ———, in the ——— regiment of ———, in the war of 1861, who———[*here state the time, place, and cause of death*].

She further declares that her said son, upon whom she was wholly or in part dependent for support, having left no widow or minor child under sixteen years of age surviving, declarant makes this application for a pension under the above-mentioned act, and refers to the evidence filed herewith, and that in the proper department, to establish her claim.

She also declares that she has not, in any way, been engaged in, or aided or abetted, the rebellion in the United States; that she is not in the receipt of a pension under the 2d section of the act above mentioned, or under any other act, nor has she again married since the death of her son, the said ———.

My post-office address is as follows: ———.

(Declarant's signature.)

Also personally appeared ———— and ————, residents of (*county, city, or town*), persons whom I certify to be respectable and entitled to credit, and who, being by me duly sworn, say that they were present and saw ———— sign her name (*or make her mark*) to the foregoing declaration; and they further swear that they have every reason to believe, from the appearance of the applicant and their acquaintance with her, that she is the identical person she represents herself to be.

(Signature of witnesses.)

Sworn to and subscribed before me, this ———— day of ————, A.D. 186-; and I hereby certify that I have no interest, direct or indirect, in the prosecution of this claim.

(Signature of judge or other officer.)

E.

FORM OF DECLARATION OF ORPHAN SISTERS FOR ARMY PENSION.

State [Territory or District] of ————,
        County of ————,   *ss.:*

On this ———— day of ————, A.D. ————, personally appeared before the ———— of the ————, A.B., a resident of————, in the county of ————, and State [Territory or District] of ————, aged ———— years, who, being first duly sworn according to law, doth on oath make the following declaration, in order to obtain a pension under the act of July 14, 1862: That he is the legally appointed guardian of [*here give the names and ages of his ward or wards*], who ———— the only surviving child ———, under sixteen years of age, of ———, and ———, his wife, and sister of———, who was a ——— in company ———, commanded by ———, in the ——— regiment of ———, in the war of 1861, who [*here state the time, place, and cause of his death*]. That the brother of his said ward—, upon whom they were wholly or in part dependent for support, having left no widow, minor child or children, or mother, declarant as guardian, and on behalf of his ward—, refers to the accompanying evidence, and such as may be found in the department, to establish her (*or their*) claim under the law above named.

He further declares that his said ward ——— not in the receipt of any pension under said act.

My post-office address is as follows: ———————.

(Guardian's signature.)

Also personally appeared ——— and ———, residents of (*county, city, or town*), persons whom I certify to be respectable and entitled to credit, and who, being by me duly sworn, say that they were present and saw ——— sign her name (*or make her mark*) to the foregoing declaration; and they further swear that they have every reason to believe, from the appearance of the applicant and their acquaintance with her, that she is the identical person she represents herself to be.

(Signature of witnesses.)

Sworn to and subscribed before me, this ——— day of ———, A.D. 186-; and I hereby certify that I have no interest, direct or indirect, in the prosecution of this claim.

(Signature of judge or other officer.)

Monthly Pay of Non-Commissioned Officers, Privates, &c.

CAVALRY AND LIGHT ARTILLERY.

Veterinary Surgeon (cavalry only)	$75 00
Sergeant Major	21 00
Regimental Quartermaster Sergeant	21 00
Regimental Commissary Sergeant	21 00
Regimental and Battalion Hospital Steward	30 00
Saddler Sergeant (cavalry only)	21 00
Chief Trumpeter (cavalry only)	21 00
First Sergeant	20 00
Company Quartermaster Sergeant	17 00
Company Commissary Sergeant (cavalry only) . .	17 00
Sergeant	17 00
Corporal	14 00
Trumpeter of cavalry (musician of light artillery) .	13 00
Farrier or Blacksmith of cavalry (artificer of light artillery)	15 00
Saddler	14 00
Wagoner	14 00
Private	13 00

ARTILLERY AND INFANTRY.

Sergeant Major	21 00
Regimental Quartermaster Sergeant	21 00
Commissary Sergeant, battalion, of regular infantry	21 00
Commissary Sergeant, regimental, of volunteer artillery and infantry	21 00
Hospital Steward, battalion, of regular infantry . .	30 00
Hospital Steward, regimental, of volunteer artillery and infantry	30 00

Principal Musicians (usually a drum major and fife major)	$21 00
First Sergeant	20 00
Sergeant	17 00
Corporal	13 00
Musician	12 00
Wagoner (of volunteers)	14 00
Private	13 00

ORDNANCE.

Sergeant	34 00
Ordnance Sergeants of posts	22 00
Corporal	20 00
Private, first class (artificer)	17 00
Private, second class (laborer)	13 00

ENGINEER SOLDIERS.
(Sappers, Miners, and Pontoneers.)

Sergeant	34 00
Corporal	20 00
Musician	12 00
Private, first class (artificer)	17 00
Private, second class (laborer)	13 00

REGIMENTAL BANDS (REGULARS).

Leader, pay and emoluments of a second lieutenant of infantry	103 50
Musician, first class	34 00
Musician, second class	20 00
Musician, third class	17 00

BRIGADE BANDS (VOLUNTEERS).
(Sixteen musicians, inclusive of leader.)

Leader	45 00

Musician, first class $34 00
Musician, second class 20 00
Musician, third class 17 00

———

Medical Cadets (with one ration in kind
 or commutation) 30 00
Hospital Steward (appointed by the Secretary
 of War, or the hospital stewards of regimental
 non-commissioned staff) 30 00
Hospital Stewards at posts or with bodies
 of troops *of more than four companies,*
 when *detailed by the commanding officer* 22 00
Other Hospital Stewards, *detailed by the
 commanding officer,* at posts or with bodies
 of troops of *less than four companies* 20 00
Hospital Matron 6 00
Female nurses of general or permanent
 hospitals, 40 cents per day 12 00
Master Wagoners, *paid by Quartermaster's
 Department* 17 00

ENLISTED MEN OF SIGNAL CORPS.

Receive the same pay of similar grades of Engineer
 soldiers.

COLORED NON-COMMISSIONED OFFICERS, PRIVATES, &C.

All Non-Commissioned Officers $7 00
Musicians 7 00
Privates 7 00
Company Under-Cooks 7 00

[All allowed, in addition, $3 per month for clothing.

White non-commissioned officers of colored troops, same pay, &c. as in white regiments.]

$1 per month is, by law, to be retained from the pay of each private soldier of the regular army until the expiration of his enlistment.

12 ½ cents per month is, by law, to be retained from the pay of every enlisted man in the regular service for support of the "Soldiers' Home."

$2 additional per month is allowed by law to every enlisted man of the regular army for first re-enlistment, and a further sum of $1 per month for each subsequent re-enlistment, if made within one month after expiration of term of service.

Pay of Non-Commissioned Officers and Soldiers from May 1, 1864, during the Rebellion.

Act of Congress approved June 20, 1864.

CAVALRY, ARTILLERY, AND INFANTRY.

Sergeant Major	$26 00
Quartermaster and Commissary Sergeant	22 00
First Sergeant	24 00
Chief Bugler	23 00
Sergeants	20 00
Corporals	18 00
Farriers, Blacksmiths, and Artificers	18 00
Musicians and Buglers	16 00
Privates	16 00

ENGINEERS AND ORDNANCE.

Sergeant Major	$36 00
Sergeants	34 00
Quartermaster and Commissary Sergeant	22 00
Corporals	20 00
Privates-1st Class	18 00
Privates-2d Class	16 00

BANDS.

Leader	75 00
Principal Musicians	22 00
Musicians	16 00

Hospital Stewards—1st Class	33 00
" " —2d Class	25 00
" " —3d Class	23 00

Note.—The law has failed to provide correspondingly for the other non-commissioned officers not mentioned in the above list. Their pay, therefore, remains unchanged, as given in the first list. Colored troops are allowed the same as white troops.

INDEX.

THE FIGURES, EXCEPT WHERE THE WORK "PAGE" IS USED,
REFER TO THE PARAGRAPHS.

THE END.